The Philosophy of Living

The Philosophy of Living

FRANÇOIS JULLIEN

TRANSLATED BY
MICHAEL RICHARDSON
AND KRZYSZTOF FIJALKOWSKI

LONDON NEW YORK CALCUTTA

This work is published with the support of
Institut français en Inde – Embassy of France in India

Seagull Books, 2022

Originally published as François Jullien, *Philosophie du vivre*
© Editions Gallimard, Paris, 2011

First published in English translation by Seagull Books, 2016

English translation © Michael Richardson
and Krzysztof Fijalkowski, 2015

ISBN 978 1 8030 9 056 6

British Library Cataloguing-in-Publication Data
A catalogue record for this book is available
from the British Library

Typeset and designed by Seagull Books, Calcutta, India
Printed and bound by WordsWorth India, New Delhi, India

To Guillem, Hélène and Laure:
this subject is for you——living

Contents

Let us speak plainly: Doesn't living elude thought?
'Sometimes I think, sometimes I live,' Valéry noted as an
adage—in fact, there would have to be a separation
between the two, impelled to the point of exclusion. Has
thought been able to get a grasp on what living *is? And,*
above all, as soon as living is found to be in peril, on the
way it suddenly stirs within us and opens us up, so silencing
everything else. One would like to express it at a stroke
in a way that would be as unforced as possible, but have
we not always garrulously gone beyond what suddenly
brings a thrill within us, so that, as soon as living is torn
from its silence, forgotten innermost depths spring up and
living suspends its evidence? The difficulty is less to do
with speaking about the beyond than with what lies here
on this side. It is vain to allow the word 'living' to be

1

ranked alongside and among all others, mingled in their throng, for it then suddenly withdraws into isolation, gathering at a stroke within itself everything that counts, brutally returning every other word to nullity. They become no more than shadows. It is a word we ordinarily see hide and vanish under others, but that here refocuses everything over it, erasing everything that is before it. What is it that suddenly collapses, opening up in panic from within as soon as the discreet implication which everything else bore ceases to be assured? And this to such a point that everything else appears to be only window dressing . . .

For living is not simply the word we find, even more than 'being', in the pit of all others; it is especially that strange word which, while having a single meaning, an initial, simple and obviate meaning that is without ambiguity, strains itself astonishingly within itself; and which keeps us tightly held and torn both by and within its polarity. Between the sense of an official meaning that is factual and elementary (to be in life, that is, not to be dead), and the same meaning but as intensive, qualitative and even as the bearer of all values (valere—to be healthy) and, therefore, as marked with infinity, 'To live—at last!' Could we ever wish for anything else? Could we imagine anything other that what might gratify our expectation at the same time as whatever is already *given to us? What could we sing about except the 'region in which to live', as Plato, but also Mallarmé, said?*

What counts here is not so much that living stretches from one to the other, from the biological to the ethical, so conferring upon us our dimension as humans, as the contradiction into which this places us: on the one hand, living is what we find ourselves in and from which there can be no retreat, in which we are always already engaged and from which we could never imagine emerging (even when we would like to die); on the other, it is what we always remain distant from, from which we are for ever in a state of lack, of withdrawal—and that we shall never attain. It is the most elementary word while also expressing the absolute—a word that is 'basic' at the same time as it leaves us most nostalgic. It expresses the condition of all conditions while also setting out the horizon of all aspirations. Could we ever dream of anything other than living? *It is a word without any possible* infra *or* beyond. *Living, therefore, expresses at once what is most immediate and that which is never satisfied: we are living, here and now, but we do not know how to gain access to it. What is it that makes living for ever already accorded to us, in other words, since well before we have just started to doubt it but which remains impossible for us.*

Does living elude us because life passes, and because we die? But I wonder. Is not this lamento *about what is fleeting too easy? Would it not be because we cannot 'suspend' time in its 'flight', as bad lyricism has so often declaimed? The fact that our strength is used up, that life is extinguished and that, hardly have we been born, or even before, death is already working within us is not in truth the most disturbing thing. Would life be just a little tolerable if we were not changing at every moment? If we always remained the same, condemned to 'be' the same, as one would like it, fixed—frozen—in our identity and with no dying, would living only be* liveable, *or at least tolerable?*

But not only does life become worn out, it also sinks. *It sinks into a room, between the walls, in activity and even in friendships, absorbed as it is by habit as well as by normality. We no longer perceive living, or it remains at a distance from us, because we cannot loosen it from this discreet plunging into what accumulates around it like an indefinable and invisible quicksand into which our activities imperceptibly become blunted and retracted—and from which we can no longer extricate ourselves to be able once more to encounter: to able once more to go towards and to get up—what is called the* drive *or the* alert. *In what is not so much the fact of a period* (durée) *as of 'duration' (in other words, that slow march of sclerosis and enclosure silently making its way below the period), and such that living is actually given to us but can no longer be attained—we can no longer effectively separate what would be the ethical from the organic: this capacity to* spring forth *withdraws without our even noticing, and the possibilities narrow. We have invented festivities, art, theatre and debauchery in order to awaken it. Morality only comes later. Where does philosophy fit in?*

The temptation has been to split it in two, *both because living is what is most elementary, what we share with the amoeba at the same time as our aspirations culminate in it, and because living thereby takes us to the point of tearing one apart from the other. Philosophy is traditionally devoted to this division: between a life that would be purely metabolic and so stupidly repetitive but that would therefore be judged to be unified, and an eternal life, one that, eluding time, unfolding into the beyond, anchored in Being and seized with verticality, a life that, shunning the former, will be called 'true life'. But once we cease to consent to the deferring of the plenitude of living into some Beyond or Later (even if it is no longer projected into some separated—hoped for—'region', or is not consequently accepted that another life is needed to support or fulfil this life here, as the only one, after it has been devalued—which is how our modernity is signalled), it will be necessary for us to conceive of the non-metaphysical tools that would allow us to grasp this absolute of living in each instant that is offered to us, something which Nietzsche ultimately, like all those who have wanted to bring life back to earth, did not formulate. In this respect, we are still today singularly deprived (which is why we consign the thought of living, when it is serious, to novels—like those of Balzac or Stendhal—or to poetry).*

Living finally *happens only in the present, as we know—it is here and now. We have ceased to be naive enough to believe that we are immediately able to take hold of the here and now. But for all that we must distrust the adverse temptation—to allow ourselves to embark upon an endless mediation, that of discourse-reason (the* logos *of philosophy) which for ever turns us away from them. Hence what I pose here is more a question of strategy than of morality. Consequently, we would be unable to* gain access *to this 'living' into which we are from the start immersed. This is why living eludes us and why we remain eternally nostalgic for it. It therefore becomes necessary to introduce divergence and distance in respect to it, so as to discover and grapple with it at the same time as to keep ourselves from letting it split up and too conveniently be divided into two.*

In this book I will examine how a way out of this impasse can be found from a number of perspectives.

How, without renouncing it, do we emerge from an immediacy that is condemned to being illusory and become sterile? How do we prevent ourselves from being engulfed in the immediacy of living without abandoning it? But how can we allow it to appear, or, rather, transpire, in the between *of its transition? And, above all, if we are to cause this* living *to emerge, let us learn to stop diluting its presence into an extended time in which we can never live.*

I

WHILE PRESENT, THEY ARE ABSENT

1

We all recognize a typical and inescapable scene which gets imperturbably repeated. But should we simply smile at it? The tourists get out of the bus; with a glance they establish what they can photograph and consign it to the can—that's it. They then exclaim, with an intake of breath as they chatter among themselves, 'How beautiful it is!' The 'beautiful' is affixed to it like a label on a parcel—as a way of clearing it away. All they then have to do is return to their seats with a sense of relief. In short, they have done everything to avoid being present at the landscape; passing through it with the best will in the world but prudently remaining apart from it. Do they have the slightest suspicion of this? In order to spare themselves the dramatic requirement of actually being there, they gaze and gaze again (but are they simply 'gazing'?), instead of allowing themselves to be seized—being divested—by whatever they have come across and by which they are suddenly overwhelmed in its miracle that could hold them in suspense, interminably, to the point of vertigo, without their being able to tear themselves away from it.

I've said that they return to the bus with a sense of relief. But what are they 'relieved' about? 'Prudence' (in the face of an ominous peril)—but why should this be? It is clear: they are relieved to have avoided a confrontation—a confrontation with what *appears* before them, devouring their attention and overflowing upon every side. Photography has provided them with a beneficial tool that allows them to sidestep that which has arisen in front of them but cannot be appropriated—it enables them to hold it at a distance, 'in check'. Or, to designate it more precisely, to sidestep that insupportable aspect of what cannot be possessed (and cannot be consumed) as represented by that fragment of landscape. I would even say, of any fragment of landscape—it is a waste of time going to Venice to take photographs (or a waste of time going a long way in order to collide with 'miracle'). As soon as there is a field, a tree, a section of road, a roof. . . . Photography has served as a screen, conveniently sheltering us from the necessity of facing what the world suddenly displays—which exhibits the common and the banal, what has been seen so often before but also, soon as we halt there, no longer slipping past it, what is unexpected and has never before been seen. It could actually cause us to yell out—that last light, during the evening, as we were leaving the forest. Stopping in the literal sense, that is, allowing all our internal ramparts (our vital defences we have reinforced so well) to give way under its irruption: affixing the Beautiful to it is already to begin circumscribing and reducing.

It will certainly be said that this sort of photography is done in order to 'keep' (as a recall, so that it can be reclaimed later, and so on). Wasn't it even necessary to be attentive and vigilant in order to choose the best viewing angle and frame it effectively? But keeping and wanting to conserve is already to protect ourselves against what suddenly assails us, just like that fragment of the landscape which, if I stop before it just for a moment, instead of arranging it from the beginning in this way, at once shakes me and has an affect on me that is almost intolerable. In the same way, as we are careful to make good choices and to frame well, this immediately diverts us from the element of the infinite which the slightest fragment of landscape contains, and which is therefore impossible to contain or select. To take a photograph is to take cover, to interpose; it exempts us from what, as in an indentation, is immediately glimpsed as irreducible and finally intrudes, bare, in sight and unrestrained. Photographs are taken in order to flee this feeling, in other words, to avoid 'being there'—*da sein*—once, at this time, which is unique, in front of this tree or field. Or, in fact, before 'any tree' or 'any field'.[1] One will then photograph in order to restore the customary swing back into the expected, the conventional, and to block off as best as one can the place from which the panic of encounter and collision could arise—in order no longer to be exposed to this peril of being next to, facing, 'pre(s)ent', here and now (or, when we photograph faces, the effect of it then escapes us). Photography (the 'souvenir photo') is the instrument that has been designed for this avoidance. Except when it is to produce a work of art (but then the aim is the inverse, which is non-consumable 'art'), this 'taking' of photos serves as a screen to deaden the shock and disorder it brings—to reduce the intrusion of an outside, the breaking open of a *present*, in order to re-establish the continuous slippage so that internal and external (the 'self' / the 'world') properly stay on either side, in their respective aloofness, with a minimum of water-tightness, without going to further trouble.

In the same way, when listeners come in and set up their tape-recorders on the desk, I warn them: 'You are doing this to avoid being present and having to listen. You believe you will be better able to make use of this account (to listen to it again at leisure, and so on) but, in fact, you are making a preliminary arrangement in such a way that you will never listen to it, so that you are never actually listening at all. Not now, since you know that you will be able to listen again at your leisure, when you want to, *ad libitum*, as many times as you like. You are therefore given a guilt-free reason to be less attentive now and to let it pass by— you have put in place a system of security. Not later, because, if (when) you listen again, it would be in the mode of what has already formed a rut, towards which you have already prepared yourself, have become used to, and from which you are at least a little immune and indifferent—whose effects you will have taken the precaution of stifling. Words fly, they say, *verba volant*. Yes, let them fly—*verba volant*, I would say—and grasp them in their flight. Too bad if you don't understand them all (anyway, what would this 'all' constitute?); too bad if some are lost, if you are condemned to forget. Accept this fleeting and incomplete quality. In any event, it is less harmful than the organized dilution of the present under the guise of preserving it.

Rest assured that this is not a matter of starting the everlasting trial of technology again from a new angle but simply of lingering on what everyone knows—that technology, in multiplying presence, atrophies it. While extending its equipment from every part, it shelters and safeguards. It safeguards us against the assault of the present, or of what I would call, in a way that is less conducive to results, its constant *assailing*. It claims to guarantee a better and better mastery of 'time', allowing us not only to go more quickly but also to more rigorously programme the future just as to conserve the past more completely, and, especially, to take our revenge over the narrowness of the present by means of a developed simultaneity. But we all know that this is a false reign, that in allowing us to do so many things at once (to walk at the same time as to listen to music, to answer the mobile phone and so on), it surreptitiously disengages us from an exacting present. It keeps us in a pale compossibility which prevents us from encountering anything—*to zap*, the word signalling this promised victory, works against the availability which it claims to aim for. This is because the present prevails, and becomes prominent, through its exclusive quality above all. If it is banal to point out what is then lost (how much less present one is, for example, when watching a film on television than when seeing it at the cinema), it is still necessary to draw out the consequences. Again, we need to withdraw this account from its platitude and start by lingering over what it points towards: presence, at the same time as it is given to us immediately (and is it not even the only immediacy?), is what it is nevertheless necessary for us to conquer—it is what we need to *gain access to*.

2

Heraclitus formulates this trenchantly: 'When fools listen, they are like the deaf, something placed in evidence through this expression: while present they are absent.' What we read here, as we separate out the sentence, is not that they have listened foolishly but that 'having listened' they still resemble 'the deaf', something which makes them 'fools'. Absent to which they are present, said Heraclitus—they *do not encounter*. They are there, physically present in the flesh, but, as they say, their minds are elsewhere, in other words, actually nowhere: dispersed, dissipated, idle, not 'awakened'. But Heraclitus refrained from developing the dualism (body/mind) which, in the early days of philosophy, has not been consummated. The mere shock of the contraries involved, 'presence' and 'absence', here undergoes neither explanation nor mediation—Heraclitus thereby spares us from the psychologism (and moralism) in which the later tradition would become bogged down. Equally, he is not saying that these fools, because they have not listened, resemble the deaf. On the contrary—they have listened but they remain deaf. 'They' refers to those whom Heraclitus elsewhere calls the *many* (*polloi*) or the *sleeping* (*katheudontes*). Isn't it the case that sleeping means neither more nor less than to withdraw temporarily from presence? Likewise, the *formulation* (*phatis*), striking as it is, is cast over them like a condemnation, simply denouncing the inconsistency of their lives through this contradiction—present, they are absent. They think they are present, but they are not. This is because they have not *attained* presence, have not satisfied its requirements.

Heraclitus makes it clear that this required capacity lies in the aptitude to 'encounter' or, more rigorously still, that it consists in what is 'as it is' within the *encounter*. Because the 'many', in contrast, 'do not,' he says, 'think about the things they encounter'; nor 'do they know them after having been taught', even though 'they think they do'. 'To fall upon', 'to encounter' (*enkurein*)—there is that upon which I 'fall', but that I risk not taking under control in my 'thinking' (*phronein*), in other words, that I risk not conceiving in this open, sudden, thrown into confusion 'as it is' of the encounter. It means, we can guess, that I am content to represent it to myself according to acquired codifications, projecting conventional images onto it, without allowing it to make an irruption or even an infraction. Heraclitus expresses this with a powerful formulation, through its reflective phrase which usually eludes translation (rendering it by 'it seems to them' or, better, 'they conceive it', 'they imagine it'). Let us read it literally: these many 'think (it) to themselves' (*heautoisi dokeouisi*) because they remain within their 'thinking', in other words, the opinion (*doxa*) they have formed about things, turning thereby in the normal circle of their thoughts and adequacy (adaptations). Prudently avoiding all confrontation, they remain incapable of making any breakthrough that would enable them to open an effective present. The Greek word does not hide the fact that such an encounter is a 'collision' (*enkuresis*— as, in Homer, one falls on the enemy troops) which I earlier called the *assailing* of the present. Thus we read in Euripides that cowards in battle are in the same situation as these 'many' or these 'fools'—once again, although 'present, they are absent'. Is not this absence in the present, in fact, equal to cowardice and renunciation?

Presence–absence, a presence but one diluted with absence—it is a question here, in the shock of contraries, of a lot more than an oxymoron, or even of a tragic placing in tension, because such is still really, in the eyes of the Greeks, what threatens life with a fall, or what sums up the difficulty of living. The Greeks, moreover, thought so well that living meant staying within the field of 'presence', not allowing oneself to sink into 'absence', that the formulation can equally well be turned around. But all the better to affirm that nothing positive can be expected except from and through presence—because only presence is precious. Let us go beyond contenting ourselves with censuring those who, 'although present, are absent'; but what is absent is itself to be rendered present—such is what is most pure about our activity; or such is the definition, for the Greeks, of what 'thinking' can mean. Parmenides, rather than going in the opposite direction to Heraclitus, as they are ordinarily characterized in relation to each other (one of them speaking of Being as immobile, the other of the 'fluency' of things), improved upon the value of presence to the point that it was the only thing he retained: 'Look upon things which, though absent, are yet firmly present in thought' (*Fragments*: Fragment 4). To think, in other words, through which life for the Greeks was to be described, means to make presence emerge, means to be kept before the spirit, to abolish absence.

Not only do I render myself effectively present, present-present and no longer present-absent, that is to say, that I no longer allow absence to erode my presence or surreptitiously undermine it, but also I will now even surmount such an opposition through thought— and such is really what thought calls for; in other words, what the spirit rises to through its capacity. Not only have I ceased to allow presence to be contaminated by absence, but also I have absorbed absence into presence. If 'to think' is to annul absence, it is because being is no longer allowed to be 'cut' from being, as was later developed; because it is no longer delivered up to the contradictory play, in continual renewal, of 'dispersion' and 'bringing together' and because, consequently, one can no longer tolerate that a singular position, whatever it might be, would on its own be able to demarcate arbitrarily, and from its local point of view, the horizon of the thinkable. Indeed, since 'to be' and 'to think' are declared to be identical with each other (ibid.: Fragment 3), and since one cannot therefore 'think' what 'is not', it is logical for the dimension of absence to disappear in thought and, consequently, for me 'firmly' to hold being in its entirety under the 'gaze' (*leussein*) of my thought. In conformity with the force of intellectual vision, virtual absences are 'equally' integrated, and all distance is dissipated. Presence/absence: What will definitively remain of such a disjunction? Must they not be held to the inertia of the spirit, one and the other, still dissociated? 'To think', through which living was accomplished in the eyes of the Greeks, means to triumph over it.

Heidegger was therefore completely justified in advancing the fact that 'to be' for the Greeks meant 'to be present' (that *einai* should be translated by *pareinai*), on which the later history of Western philosophy is founded, even if it means that such a 'presence' would remain unthought (Heidegger 1998). This is because 'being' would otherwise still remain that empty, inept and undetermined word, equivalent just as much to its opposite, the 'nothingness' of non-being denounced by Hegel. But looking at the Greeks is especially invaluable (do we have to be reminded of it?) in that it detaches this experience of lived being as presence from what metaphysics has abstractly made of it. This has tended to fix (congeal) presence in permanency and, under the pale spectre of interminable duration, to confuse being itself with subsistence and, by the same token, substance, having become inert because essentialized (become *ousia*). Due to this, metaphysics has been led to misunderstand presence in its growth and sudden springing up (*Anwesung* and no longer *Anwesenheit*. See Heidegger 1939)—as an abrupt irruption which brings about an event. It is no longer conceived according to the horizontality of a temporal extent that would define its constancy, but is experienced according to the pressure of a break-through and an emergence.

Indeed, have we not, under the weight of the present that had become a constant of metaphysics and which uniformly outlined existence, been led to forget this 'dawning' of presence—at once divulging itself of absence and reviving itself through its withdrawal? But when one suddenly runs into some fragment of landscape, instead of limiting oneself to photograph-ing it, or, encountering these three trees at a bend in the road when taking an alternative route, one tackles them instead of mechanically avoiding them, that is when the present immediately opens up. Whether one allows this presence to occur through its resolu-tion or, as Heraclitus said, an 'awakening' operates in the *as it is* of the encounter—the 'present' is this *resolution*.

3

A resolution to do what? Let us say, *not to defer*. It is
the resolution not to postpone to (a falsely fleeting
later on) which alone opens a real present. Whether
it is a question of the two Martinville church towers
revealed in the setting sun, at the bend in the road,
appearing, disappearing then reappearing, to which
will incidentally be added that of Vieuxvicq, or of the
young lady walking towards the station on a path illuminated by the dawn light, carrying her milk jug to
the travellers, or simply of the three trees at the
entrance to an alleyway (see Proust 1992a), the discovery and the shock are the same. From what suddenly comes into our presence a 'special pleasure'
arises, as Proust tells us, returning all the others to a
shared pallor and throwing us into confusion. Finally,
in this *as it is* of the encounter, we no longer substitute
for it that 'standard convention' which we form day
after day as we make a sort of average of 'different
faces which have pleased us', as Proust says, or 'the
pleasures we have known' at the core of our being, and
which over the years weave a sort of personal *doxa*
that spreads over everything, or parasitical 'thinking',
as Heraclitus said, under whose shelter we deaden life.

But for all that is it necessary, as the author of *In
Search of Lost Time* would have it, to 'go to the limit'

of this sudden impression, to seek out something which would be 'behind'—behind this movement or lucidity—something 'secret' and whose 'envelope' it would be best to open, whose 'bark' we should tear off? Would this not be the remains of the metaphysic but to which Proust, moreover, had greater recourse perhaps, here, in order to underline, to affirm so much more strongly that the present is to be penetrated, to be invested, to be broken into and not to be allowed to slip away? For can it be protected in its phenomenality without assuming some hidden essence in it? Why, in order to enhance it, fall into the conventional language of Revelation and endow it with mystery? And, in the same way, do we need the hope of returning here one day, taking the same train, as the Narrator allows himself to, deluding ourselves with the idea that we will be able to live alongside this young lady and accompany her then, without having to leave her again, in all of her daily tasks? I ask: Why, in order to secure this time, should we invent the fiction of another time? Why not be satisfied with the uniqueness of the encounter instead of wanting to protect, to extend, to conserve—a discreet way of always escaping from it?

This did not prevent Proust from concluding each of his scenes with what is most important—the effort needed in order *to gain access* to the present and deploy its 'intoxication'. And then, as is right, if we are no longer to assume a world beyond this world or a backdrop to these sudden breakthroughs, if we are not to rest on the idea of a possible doubling of their being and appearance, still more tenacity and attention is required. 'A painful obligation', as Proust put it, but to 'comply with an enthusiasm'—to emerge from that ordinary existence, 'reduced to a minimum', in which we live. Thanks to the interruption of routine on a morning of travel, profiting from the change of place and time, 'dormant' faculties become mobilized and their 'presence' suddenly becomes 'indispensable'; my 'being in its entirety' is summoned for a challenge, without being allowed the luxury of any suspicion or dualistic scorn—the disturbance involved goes from respiration and 'appetite' right up to the 'imagination'.

Nevertheless, the temptation, as Proust warns, is really to allow that assailing moment to escape once more, to integrate it immediately into the same measure as the others, not to be satisfied with what becomes evident but to let these two church towers 'join again all those many trees, roofs, perfumes and sounds I have distinguished from others due to the obscure pleasure they have given me and that I have never deepened'. Moreover, in his book, one word (in the mouth of Saint Loup) expresses this postponing of present being to a later time, in other words, that way of avoiding taking in hand what suddenly becomes one's responsibility: 'procrastination'—one postpones 'until tomorrow'.... But obviously, and no one has ever doubted this, to postpone this con-fronting of the encounter is definitively to miss the possibility of the present which is offered—a 'present' being understood aptly in French (as in English) in two ways—as both a given moment and a gift.

This peril is well known to everyone—to conjure away the present happens in all processes as in all moments. Even if only now, when I read, because when I read, the temptation to *postpone* is that I can reread. In the same way when I write—I can correct. I count on the fact that hardly has this sentence been completed than I can go back to it, thereby allowing myself a reduced and enfeebled presence to what I do—one that is less vigilant. Or, to bring into play once more this shock of contraries, now reading but already assuming that I will reread, I am 'present-absent'. In other words, I count upon the fact that I can redo in order not to do; that I can reread in order not to read. The appearance of the second time allows me to step across the first time, and no time ever happens—I am already awaiting the next sentence in order to relieve me of the previous one and follow the reading in a continual slippage and avoidance of what I need to confront. I thereby evade the shock of the encounter, that of an unpredictable meaning and its exigency—by *postponing*, I am taking precautions against a too-violent throwing into confusion, that is to say, that I elude the actual effort of taking responsibility through the promise of afterwards being better able, in a second effort, to assume it. But to what point can I really be taken in by this? It is the laziness of 'I will return to it'.

This is because when I immediately reread a sentence, I go back to a meaning that is already deadened, more or less arranged, adopted and assimilated and therefore also diffused, in short, a meaning which I have started to strip of its strangeness, which I have already caused to capsize into the beginnings of a habitual and comfortable familiarity. For all that, does this mean I grasp it more effectively? Is it better understood due to the fact that it is less puzzling? Even underlining, making notes in the margin or highlighting the text are already appeals to the later, they are ways of postponing (of resting), they are already escapes—an indication that one wants to conserve so as to evade the encounter. By going back in advance to the possibility of a rereading, I have sheltered myself without remorse from the discovery and its event. And I concur, by a sort of past tacit agreement with myself, with a certain (and even henceforth legitimate) tolerance of 'absence' or inattention, in other words, on a diluted present.

4

To define the present by 'attention' is, in fact, amply anchored in the history of philosophy. Let us see if this conception is sufficient: Would *attention* alone constitute the present? Let us recall the fundamental difficulty the Greeks encountered in thinking about 'time'. Conceiving it, like everything else, in terms of 'being', they were driven to the assertion that the future does not yet 'exist', that the past no longer 'exists' and that the present, being only the point at which the future becomes the past, has no greater extension than a point (a purely geometrical point), and so, consequently, it has no phenomenal existence. Admittedly, it will be said, time must exist since it can be divided into 'past', 'present' and 'future'. Yes, but these divisions do not exist (it is a *mériston* with no *méré*), as Aristotle recognized. Time would therefore be of 'obscure' existence (*amudrôs*). In relation to this, Augustine effected a major turning point. Approaching this temporal problematic from the new existential perspective, that is, the Christian relation to God, he effected the emergence of the constitutive figure of the Self-Subject; thus, from this distension and separation of the three parts of time, we must seek existence only within ourselves, in our minds; it is a *distentio animi*. These three times correspond in fact to three activities: the future is what I 'await'; the past is what I 'remember'; and the present is that to which I am 'attentive' (*attendo*). It is therefore defined *stricto sensu* as 'attention' (*Confessions*: 11.28.37. I refer in this respect also to Jullien 2001: Chapter 4).

It remains the case that Augustine found himself once more in a tight spot when he wanted to find his place within this 'attention' constituting the present, caught as this was between the two expansive modalities, each as dominant as the other, of expectation (of the future) and memory (of the past). Did not the former transmute itself (did it not decant itself) almost directly into the latter? What margin or what fissure, what (impossible) decree for an intermediary (the transition of the present), can such an *almost* tolerate? What chink emerges from between these two dispositions, expectation and memory, master activities, rivals, forming a polarity, 'where' an 'attention' (characteristic of the present) could emerge? All the more so since any true 'where' lies Elsewhere.

Just as he thinks through, indeed, this difference of times beginning from the system of questions of place in Latin (the place 'from which' one comes—*unde*: the future), 'towards which' one is going (*quo*: the past), 'through which' one passes (*qua*: the present), this present is always, for Augustine, only the 'point' of passage, without extension and therefore without existence, of the future 'flying' into the past—the final case, the place 'where one exists' (*ubi*), being reserved for where God is, since He alone 'exists'—no longer in 'time' but in 'eternity'. This no longer relates to our 'at-tention' (in the 'nearness' of the 'pres'-ent) but our 'in-tention' (*in-tentio*), the only truly intensive mode, extending us entirely towards Him, by converting us, to find Him again. It will require all the finesse of Husserl's phenomenological analysis, reconsidering that of Augustine, to extend this fleeting attention, even if only to the dimensions of a melody to which one listens, such an attention then straining itself between the 'pro-tension' towards the sounds immediately to come and the 're-tension' of sounds only just released and dissipating, but 'like the tail of a comet', into the past (Husserl 1964; 1991).

The Husserlian analysis nevertheless confers extension on attention, by *pro* and *re*-tension, and, consequently, gives existence to the present only in dependency on a temporal object (*Zeitobjekt*) like the melody. And is it not effectively condemned always to demand this 'objective' support, without which such an attention loses its pertinence—and therefore presence its consistency? The evidence is the parallel we read in Bergson. When, considering that this attention can be prolonged or shortened as we wish, like the space between two points of a pair of compasses, he envisages that such attention to the present could hold under its gaze 'in addition to my last phrase', that which preceded it and even all the earlier phrases, therefore that it could be 'indefinitely extendible', rendering thereby, if not in an arbitrary then at least in a relative way, the distinction we make between our present and our past (the 'present' occupying, he tells us, 'exactly as much space as this effort'). Bergson arrived in this way at the notion of 'attention to life', stretching out in duration, which 'would embrace', in an 'undivided present', the whole of the past. But, look—he then fatally lapses into the conditional and condemns himself to a pious wish (Bergson 1984: 1386–92). And he sinks, at the same time, into bad lyricism (the song of a 'perpetual present')—our perception 'is heated up', 'everything' is revived within us, he promises us, we 'live more'. . . . An awkward but inevitable fall, in the end, as soon as we forsake the support of the temporal 'object', in a drifting subjectivism, given over to auto-suggestion and becoming garrulous, spinning like a freewheel since we no longer have anything upon which to grip. How to free oneself from this?

This is why I intend to break with the atavistic conception of a present *by extension*, whether this should come from our 'attention', or even more ostensibly from our 'action', such as sensation seizes it, as the Stoics already understood it—for Chrysippe, the present is as long as a walk when I am walking. Where does an act begin, or end (the 'act' being distinguished from the perceived action)? If the present, as the point of emergence of duration, is indefinitely reducible, time itself being divisible to infinity (something which has never ceased to worry us), I *open onto* the present, in contrast, and make it emerge as soon as I put up an obstruction to the temptation to *postpone*. As soon as I cease to assume that what happens will return, as soon as I attach myself to this occurrence without seeking its before or after, not so much because of its possible rarity (a 'beautiful' landscape) as for what emerges within it that is irreducibly unique, it is then that a 'landscape' (like the church towers of Martinville) is made effective.

If, therefore, *attention* is insufficient to constitute the present, both because it remains dependent on that to which it is attentive and because its extent is not clear but frayed, *not to postpone* depends, in contrast, as a decision, only on itself, and, from the beginning, inscribes a stumbling block. Not to postpone raises an obstruction (in the haemorrhagic course of 'time') on this side of which a present can accumulate—'a' present, and not the present. Let us say that as soon as I cease to defer I am anchored in a present. It is a present that 'takes' as a fire takes, alights, sets itself up (bestows itself) and is consumed. For if it is not of an extensive order (what 'interval' of duration? is the question that has always been asked), it is, logically, an *intensive*, and the *intensio* which Augustine reserved for eternity needs to be transferred onto it, or it does not possess the quantitative except through the qualitative. From that point I take the instant out of the unstable and promote it to its opposite, maintaining the *as it is* of the encounter and the confrontation.

Let us simply recall that the word 'now', 'maintenant', is made up from *manu tenere*, 'to hold by the hand' and 'maintain'.[2] 'We never stay in the present time,' said Pascal harshly. In short, this would be the opposite of the Nietzschean eternal return though it touches upon it in its aim. It is the contrary not always

31

but one time, *semel*, which can be only a single time. With, nevertheless, the same effort (effect) in mind— there is a present only by the decision (resolution) to assume. I no longer seek to retain, to make it return or last, to the point that the 'ephemeral', that old foundation of every complaint and of all lyricism, would no longer be deplorable.

5

For all that, could this satisfy us? This demand for a *non-postponement* calls for another which appears to be its opposite but is just as much its complement. A necessary complement—it is in the day or the play which opens up between them, and which unmakes what would otherwise prematurely be taken to be a paradox, that we deploy life. On the one hand, it is said, I refuse to postpone and thereby I do not claim to 'suspend' time in its 'flight', according to the bombastic wish of the poet, but no less do I make the present appear as soon as I approach it as a *moment*. This is because a 'moment' really comes from 'movement' (*momentum* from *movimentum*), but not as what is measured (in length) but, rather, as what is dug out and filled in. With what, then, can a moment be filled if not by presence? Its capacity comes from what it can contain, at times to the point that its content appears to overflow. For Proust, the event (of amorous disturbance) is not entirely maintained in the moment in which it takes place. A moment no longer has a beginning and an end but crosses thresholds and degrees, according to its intensification. It enhances itself as it detaches itself, breaks with its surroundings, is in retreat from the ordinary, emphasizes its quality (even that so banal 'precious moment') and falls back onto its uniqueness—a moment is always singular and, to the extent that it is made of an unbiased encounter, in other words, of a confrontation, it arises effectively from what is voluntary. 'The moment of' (leaving, acting, cutting . . .)—the formulation is then an injunction. Hence this *refusal of postponement* shading into the moment by anticipation and depending on what comes next, instead of presence being gathered up in its cavity—but, from another side, which, aiming at contradiction, will counterbalance presence, and so, opening between them a breach by which to live, I accept what is *differed*.

I do more than accept. If I count on the *differed*, it means that I am not limited to my aim, that I give 'time some time', that I know how to wait for a materialization which no longer belongs to me. I divest myself of impatience in order to gather. To be able to 'gather' (according to the well-known, hackneyed

33

carpe diem), does this not already need to have been allowed, somewhere, to *ripen*? This implies that I do not confine myself to my role as a voluntary subject but that I know how to recognize that a process, which escapes me, is at work and already within myself, already in my mind—a course has been primed which no longer depends on 'me'; an operativity has been introduced which 'makes its way', as they say, discreetly relieving 'me', without an account of it being given or even dreamt of, and this, even if it is within myself that it is produced, if it is me, a 'subject', whom it concerns.

To agree with the differed means that I consider the present moment to be an investment. Financiers speak in their jargon, but it is a strong language insofar as it sticks to what is effective (the concern with a yield), of a 'return on the investment'. Or, it will be better still to speak of a return to immanence. At the same time as I confront this time existing here, the time that I want only once, then already, without realizing it, I am in the process of investing and capitalizing. Then, one day, 'it comes', by way of result, 'all alone', *sua sponte*—'that' makes its breakthrough, deploys its effect by itself: 'encounters'. Its subject is no longer 'me' but the process engaged upon. Indefinite but also deictic—'that'. Undetermined because not anticipated, not framed, an expiry I cannot reckon upon. At the same time, this consequence suddenly becomes obvious before my eyes, resulting from who knows where but henceforth completely obvious after having escaped me.

'That happens,' they say. But what is 'that'? Each time, as though it was the only time, I practice, I do my scales, I do my utmost—no effect; the fumblings of the effort and the clumsiness can still be noticed. Some time passes, I have stopped thinking about it. Then, one morning, opening the piano again, I find that I am amazingly at ease in playing the sonata, as though it was given to me. What subterranean work had taken place, through the days, whose 'present' is there? Or, again: not 'I think', but from where does thought come (to me)? From what night has it been hatched? For my thought itself, which I believe self-sustainingly (stoically) governs (my freedom), is a process of silent transformations and maturations whose coherence escapes the causality of the Subject that 'I am' (an accurate Nietzchean critique of the *cogito*, such a 'subject' discovering itself as a process (see Nietzsche 1968b: 1, §147–8). The evening before, I had sought my words and ideas with difficulty and without getting anywhere. And then, when I awake the next day, the page is written, imposing itself on me as if by an encounter and causing an irruption—as though it was dictated to me (it will be said: 'inspired').

Let us return to the example of reading, or, rather, recognize that it involves *two* rereadings. We will lazily refuse, when reading, to postpone the present of the reading by immediately rereading it to make good its absence. But, time having flowed by, the book being put aside and even forgotten, when we reread we do not simply renew the past reading and recall it. This is because the rereading has profited behind the scenes from an infinity of connections that elude me, finally imposing, in a clear, effective and non-scrambled way, what I could earlier only discern with difficulty—as though the reading of it had never ceased to develop in silence, so that this text, decanted of what had choked or interfered with its approach, finally releases its 'significance'. Having passed through a time of forgetting (false forgetting, for the memory working surreptitiously), I discover it this time more originally (radically), grasping more of its fundamentals and amazing myself with all the things I had not read in it. The rereading is thus no longer laziness but a progress as unhoped for as it is unperceived.

More subtle than the art of doing (immediately, by exerting oneself) is that of the *allowing to happen* (counting on a ripening)—when the subject places his initiative between parentheses in order to allow the progress that is underway to operate in concert and over a longer period. When this disengagement is not for all that a renunciation (nor is this withdrawal a falling back into irresponsibility, or this non-activism a fall back into passivity), when the faculties provoked are put on ice in order for the implied factors and conditions to be more broadly mobilized and to come together to unblock a difficulty encountered, the instant confrontation of which would be heroic but of little effect. Duration unravels on its own. As a matter of fact, this 'so that' I have advanced is itself to be corrected, marked with too much finality—it cannot have aimed there, and it is what renders the causing to (allowing to) happen to be so delicate and *in such a way* that it would be the very *moment* which finally, more impersonally, would be able to deliver the effect without its being projected.

This implies giving credit to the virtue of the unfolding. And perhaps it is why contemporary society is drawn to neglect such a value of the *differed* (and that, for example, education, which necessarily counts on the differed, is rendered so difficult). A culture like the current one, always anticipating more and consequently throwing itself towards targets while giving in to the fascination of 'real time' (provided by the technology of communication), misunderstands the generous contribution made by delay. Yet a civilization (like the individual) is strong only at the level of the differed it can bear, that is, in what a generation knows how to plant (as a resource to come) without claiming to be able itself to harvest it—I will not see the shade of the oaks with which I have reforested the hill. Is not the same thing true in politics?

6

Likewise, when I spoke about how the refusal of the one (the postponement) and the acquiescence to the other (the differed) opened a space in which to manoeuvre (that *differed* and *postponed*, far from being entirely synonyms, allow us to see the play between them from which life can be deployed), it was a question above all of emphasizing this—that living is perhaps not so much a matter of morality as of strategy, 'good' and 'evil' being themselves, we know, only derived categories, representing a more ideal, or social, choice, than a properly effective one. I understand that living is 'strategic', in the sense that an operational capacity is liberated within it which, thinking itself in step with the situation being confronted, can have in view the maximum of effect in exploiting one as well as the other—not to skew the present encountered as well as letting it bear fruit.

This leads us to consider both at the same time: to respond to the *instance* of the present, that 'instant' which goes beyond being understood as an exigency rejecting the repetition-conservation; but, equally, to allow the immanence and its capacity for giving birth to operate. This can also arise as an alternative and lead us to a decision: Am I in the process of evading it *or* of allowing it to come, of avoiding the confrontation of the encounter and, consequently, missing the occurrence of the present and the plenitude of the moment it offers? Or, rather, is it that I do not postpone, but nor do I force, that I do not avoid, but that in letting it rest I do so in such a way that a deposit silently accumulates, from which the present becomes 'perennial'—'the virgin, perennial, and the beautiful today' ('La vierge, le vivace et le bel aujourd'hui'; Mallarmé 1994: 67) can have unexpected results?

Chinese language, with no conjugations, cannot mark different times, but retains the verbal function in that sole form that would be for us the infinitive. Equally, it does not distinguish between the active and passive voices, and readily avoids expressing a grammatical subject, implicitly preserving it within the phrase, nor does it play on the opposition between 'being' and 'non-being', of existence and nothingness. Its principal categories are those of the 'flow' and of the energy invested or in the 'capacity' (*dao* and *de*), and there is less within it to give expression to the relation of means to end, or intention it principally relates conditions to consequences (the 'root' and the 'branches', *ben—mo*). For all these reasons, Chinese thought is particularly at ease in evoking the operative as it develops, advancing in silence, and which one learns to use, harnessing it like a 'spring' but without being able for all that to govern it. *Dao* ('*tao*'), the master-word of this thinking, expresses at once the self-deployment of this immanence and the art of making use of it, the processes and the procedure—the *dao* of the world and 'my' *dao*. Thus it is said in it, taking all schools together, that it is necessary to know how to allow the effect to occur, as a consequence, or a 'return', of a preliminary investment, confident that one is in the propensity under way and acquiescing wisely in this differed—rather than worrying the world with one's desire and impatience. And, in its Taoist aspect, the attitude of disinterest and detachment is highlighted more fully which, unlike interest, leads in a 'natural' way (*ziran*) to this culmination.

A text like the *Laozi* (also known as *Te-tao Ching*) thereby thinks without difficulty about what we call *morality* in terms of strategy: 'The wise man

starts at the back' in such a way that he would be able
to be 'carried ahead'. Not due to modesty or a vow of
humility but because, choosing to situate himself
within the hollow, he calls upon the effect to realize
himself fully (§7). This *differed* is itself the bearer of
effect. Rather than want the result from the outset
through his action, it is better to discreetly set in train
a process which leads there *of itself*—and such is the
art of 'not acting' (*wu wei*). If we were to seek the
result immediately, we would straightaway place ourselves at the terminal state of the process and, consequently, already be situated at the point at which we
see the process reverse, therefore putting ourselves in
peril (§9). Instead of 'keeping a tight hold on it', it is
better to stop as early as possible in order to prepare
the field for the event *sua sponte* of the effect which,
proceeding from its own maturation and carried along
by conditions, will be so much better implanted and,
consequently, more solid. For it finds itself progressively
implicated by the situation, in proportion to its development, and is no longer a forcing.

The *Laozi* says this tersely, but without there
being a paradox: 'partial, from which the complete
comes; curved, from which the straight comes; hollow,
from which the full comes' (§22). We cannot directly
aim at the complete, the 'straight' or the 'full'; but, by
situating ourselves in the inverse state, the hoped-for

effect is allowed to be adopted ('naturalized') by the continuing course of things and to extend by itself to its dawning. 'From which' (*ze*) means this relation of condition to consequences, and it makes clear the implication of the unfolding. What we ordinarily (subjectively) take to be the virtue of patience is, in fact, only the benefit drawn from what is *differed* which has been allowed to work. Indeed, in a still more offensive mode: 'If one wants to weaken, it is first of all necessary to reinforce; if one wants to eliminate one must first promote; if one wants to remove, one must first grant', and so on. A political translation (according to Wang Bi): rather than beat a tyrant, let him tyrannize to the point at which he will finally undermine his own position through this excess and destroy himself . . .

I have translated this as 'it is first', but the Chinese says, more correctly—in an 'inherent', 'immanent', 'intrinsic' way (*gu*). Such is what is called, says the *Laozi*, the *subtle intelligence* (*wei ming*). In taking the idea so far, that one is implicated in the other and assumes existence only through it, will this not undermine in return the field of the pertinence, or the 'as for the self' (*kath' hauto*, as the Greek said), of each? If no determination coincides any longer with itself, but finds its point of departure in its opposite, what can 'being' still signify? This would lead us to ask, consequently, if the Chinese, who have not thought in terms of 'being' but of process, have not been better qualified to think about the phenomenon of life, since life is a process. And perhaps it is necessary, in fact, to get down to that point, into the thinking of processivity, in order to finally see the undermining of the great opposition of 'presence' and 'absence' that gives Being its meaning, to which the West, ever since the Greeks, has been so firmly attached, even Heraclitus and his well-known 'everything flows'.

II

THE EVIDENCE AND THE WITHDRAWAL

1

The idea that the festivities (*fête*) occurs 'before the festivities' is not simply a theme for schoolchildren when they are starting to learn how to debate. If the remark is trivial, then what does it signal towards? If the festivities occur before the festivities, as we said, what this means is not simply that the anticipation might be more beautiful than the reality, or that we might live more by the imagination than by what 'is true', in short, that any festivity might be disappointing in relation to what we expected of it. Admittedly, we can hardly be satisfied with this and remain at such a psychological level. Let us, rather, unravel the threads of what is revealed in a banal way in order to see what lies behind it. Are we not divulging a more essential *non-coincidence*, which on its own could enable us to think through what living is? If the festivity does not coincide with the 'festivity' and is lost when it is set out; if, when we say 'this is the festivity', it no longer really is a festivity, then this relates to some coherence, perhaps even verifies itself at every turn, but it still does not escape from logic (from the 'logic' of *logos*). Not that I might be the one not to know how to be contemporary with the festivity, but, rather, that it is really the festivity which, when it faithfully produces all the signs attesting to the 'festivity', cannot be contemporary with itself in the way it surges up. This is because when the *marks* (*Merkmal*, as logicians would say) by which the 'festivity' is defined are realized, and occur in a positive way, it may no longer entirely be festivity, revealing sufficiently well that it escapes such marks in the way it springs up; that what within it is effective—at once drive and energy—is removed from that positivity; consequently, it finds itself lost in its definition. The festivities have already withdrawn from these tangible marks into which they have settled and which determine them.

Let us therefore recognize how to take a momentary halt at this triteness, not scorning this banality. When we say that someone is 'virtuous', someone whom we recognize and thereafter describe as such, do we not equally suspect, in a certain way, that he has already ceased to be virtuous, that despite fulfilling all the requirements of virtue, he no longer satisfies them? The evidence for it is contained in those cautious quotations marks by which we take hold of such a modifier and which are enough to express the fact that by ostensibly detaching the statement from us, we indicate that we are not taken in by it. 'Virtue', by differentiating and assigning itself, making it identifiable and defining it, is revealed at the same time to be determined and, due to this fact, bound, sealed, stiffened and marked. This is already *agreed upon* on the way to this stereotype. The fecundating, overflowing, insolent-inspiring generosity, which *effectively* creates virtue, is withdrawn from what it has as application as it verifies itself meticulously from one act to the next. Whoever is called *virtuous* (about whom we consider saying 'he is virtuous') is no longer, as everyone knows apart from ourselves, anything but someone in need of virtue—whatever can be described (or labelled) is losing its capacity. Similarly, about someone who is said to be *pious*, who is designated as such, this means precisely that this quality has been isolated and made to stand out, for we know beforehand that piety is sad, dull, tight and stingy, confined in its features. His merit is effectively constituted solely from the fact that it has allowed him to be enclosed within these tangible marks, that it has lost this impetus (drive) that is deployed without object or intention and that is so extensive that it cannot be retrieved from it.

According to what has been recovered from tombs, and appearing today the most authentic version, we see the *Laozi* begin with these words:

Superior virtue is not virtuous,
which is why it is virtue;
inferior virtue has not departed from virtue,
which is why it is without virtue (§38).

If such a formulation carries us from the outset to the edge of contradiction, even challenges in a resolute way the presumed principle of non-contradiction as the predicate is turned over twice against its subject, there is for all that no paradox (or abstruse or mystical thought). But the capacity at work, we are warned right away, is to be considered in a divergent way, even as far away as could be from its tangible marks—it does not allow itself to be reduced to the characteristics or properties which serve to define it and by which we see it show itself. Not that what thereby makes us suspect 'virtue' would be the opposition of appearance to being, indeed that one could tax it with hypocrisy—

this expected dividing in two is not pertinent. For, far from the 'virtuous' man being suspected of being virtuous only in appearance, it is, rather, the inverse—he sticks too closely, too assiduously, to virtue (he does not 'give it up'), is riveted to it and attaches himself so consciously to what is defined as an ideal of virtue, thereby generating acts of virtue so easily identifiable and consequently praiseworthy, that it leads him to miss what effectively constitutes an inexhaustible bursting forth of virtue.

The non-coincidence is therefore between what I would call, in order to oppose them, the *effective* and the *determinative*; between the capacity at work such that, as it springs up, it overflows and defeats any possible determination; and the determination that codifies and as such serves the definition which is henceforth completely definable and thus specifiable. For at this stage of designation, nothing more remains in it than a parcelling out of particular, completely settled, determinitives which, in their meticulous labelling, are found to be cut from their intense ground, amputated from their emergence (see Jullien 2006: Chapter 5).

An inherent property (*propre*) of what isexpressed, *logos* (and, above all, of the principle of non-contradiction which is its initial axiom), is to assign to an object the characteristic that belongs to it, assuming its properties, in other words, the determinations it would possess 'by right' and which would form its 'being', thereby conveniently placing it on the path towards knowledge. We can see that the *Laozi*, from the start, takes the opposite direction. But what other path does it open? It is not so much the 'flowing' character of things which goes against the definition (according to the old 'Heraclitean' Greek argument of 'mobility'), making an individual fail and changing him, both of which are ineffable, under the stability that language is led to veneer over things, making them properly 'things'. No, but rather this more fundamental fact—that the determination (any determination) grasps what is *settled* and not the *springing up*; that the definition is situated downstream rather than upstream, in a state of flatness that is sterile and not fecund. The state of what has already been completely developed and spread out is therefore already in the process of depletion (already has ceased to exist)— true virtue cares nothing for virtue, as true eloquence cares nothing for eloquence. The definition (codification) grasps the capacity of things even though it is already being lost. This allows living to be perceived and detached analytically into properties or qualities, because they are *already* in the process of isolation and renegotiation. Definition grasps 'being' in its coincidence but not the process by which this capacity emerges. Hence the source of the springing up, as the *Laozi* teaches, is always *in retreat*.

When a country fully shows off its strength, is even designated as strongest, or is, in any case, recognized at the summit of its power, at its apex, its strength is already wilting: the processes of decline are already being announced—history ceaselessly bears witness to this fact. There is a non-contemporaneous quality between the visible marks of the effect on the one hand, and its source (the 'mother', as the *Laozi* says) on the other. The manifestation is resultative and therefore has already been surpassed. What is effective lies in the propensity—while what is left to be recognized and identified as such (the 'such' of the essence, which the definition expresses), in its settled and labelled state, has discreetly started to go into reverse. This is the sense in which I understand another formulation from the *Laozi*:

> *Everyone knows the beautiful as beautiful, and*
> *already it is ugly;*
> *Everyone knows the good as good, and already*
> *it is not good* (§2).

Not only is what is recognized as 'beautiful', or as 'good', and which serves to define it, already on the path that will lead to its wilting, but also it constitutes something against which a new beautiful and new values, without being completely expressible or identifiable, are in the process of being devised. All those who participate in the renewal of art or poetry know this. It is why they have to remain unrecognized or contested for so long.

From this the consequence also has to be drawn—if the state of the manifested culmination is already that of wilting, then the effective plenitude is logically deficient at its source. 'Superior virtue' (in advance) does not yet offer the marks of virtue; rather, it appears 'to have a lack of them', as the *Laozi* consistently recognizes—it is said to be hollow 'like a vale' (§41). Or, again, 'great achievement is as if lacking', 'great plenitude is as if empty' (§45), or 'great eloquence' is as if 'babbling'. Let us pause once more at this 'as if'—far from indicating an intentional illusion or the deception of an appearance, this *as if* shows how this fundamental capacity necessarily shows through back to front (implicitly) when it emerges at the level of the tangible. But this is also why, it is added, 'it is not exhausted through use'—since it has taken care to settle and impose itself, it remains in retreat; nor it does not allow itself to be consumed. As evidence, we know very well the value of the sketch in painting (but precisely how long has it taken us to recognize it in Europe?)—there might be, according to Baudelaire, paintings which are 'done' but not 'finished' (while there is so much, unfortunately, which is 'finished' but not 'done'...). For what the sketch reveals against the ontological tradition (which claims that the more something is determined, the more it 'is') is that the work is all the more effective when it knows how to remain upstream, and maintain itself in process—that it takes its departure before the end so as to remain at work, that it does not conclude itself in order not to be settled. To bring a work to 'a conclusion', as Picasso said, is like putting an end to a bull—to kill it.[5]

2

I would therefore call *settling* that inverse moment of the springing up, where everything that has reached the completion of its development is patent and *coincident*—that of the definition and the expression, *logos*. But is it for all that truth? Where everything is completely offered, is evident and saturating, but, because of this, is no longer at work; consequently, thereby, as on the canvas, it is certainly *seen* but it *no longer appears*. This immobile face-to-face, no longer offering an angle, no longer revealing engagement, is sterilized—a 'finished' painting (one which is no longer *in process*). A settled sea—the tide has ceased to rise and is not yet going out. 'The sea was settled,' said Hugo, 'but the flow back began to make itself felt.' Yes, it is in fact necessary for the flow back to begin to make itself felt in order that this settling can make an appearance—for the retreat to begin to operate, even if only discreetly, so that such evidence might emerge. A ship is equally said to be settled—in a dead calm; when it neither advances nor moves back.

So may three o'clock in the afternoon, when the intensification of the morning has worn itself out and the reorientation of the evening has not yet appeared, when, in the full light of day, things are entirely settled and totally definable, at the height of their designation, without any further obscurity to threaten them or haziness to open them up to a nebulous distance. There is no further obliqueness or strategy possible in their regard—they sink into lethargy. With the day no longer being deployed yet not having withdrawn, all things are equally brimful, at the peak of their determination. They no longer betray insufficiency by being dependent on what came before, but rest perfectly in their 'property' or quality, allowing all parts to be equally delimited; this is why they no longer distinguish themselves. The very fact of the completeness of their evidence means that we no longer have a perspective on them, nor *access* to them; in consequence, we can admittedly see them, and even see nothing but them, but we no longer perceive them (something that is not at all a paradox, or at least is one that has started to dissolve). In the same way, according to Saint Augustine, the entire Creation, Heaven and Earth, endlessly proclaims the evidence of God in all its parts and at every moment and yet we do not hear it (*Confessions*: 11.4). Thus God necessarily withdraws from this world in order to be able to appear in it—for His omnipresence to be experienced, He is constrained to absent Himself.

It will therefore be advisable to oppose these two moments: the evidence (of the settling) and the withdrawal whose *evidence* is no longer discerned, and the *withdrawal* which makes an appearance. On the one hand, in the evident state of settling (of the settled sea, or of virtue recognized, of what is marked as beautiful, and, above all, of the festivity expanding in celebration . . .), what is already lost must be suspected, go back from the settling to the emergence / springing up—to return from those characteristic marks that form a definition to whatever it is of which these marks are the settling and the loss and which have already withdrawn from it. In other words, that it is appropriate to perceive, beneath the settling, that from which this settling, in its flat evidence, is the withdrawal. To such a point that this very evidence, saturating everything, no longer allows anything to infiltrate and, doing away with all access, becomes invisible to it. On the other hand, it is in the opposed moment, the one of withdrawal, that the settling is exposed, so that, emerging from its evidence, it appears. At the moment of withdrawal, there begins a desaturation of the determination which disencumbers it and takes away its opaqueness. With the reduction of presence, as absence begins to cross it, from the spreading out over distance, is illuminated, as a result, what was too evidently given, settled, discovered, in order to make ready some development, so giving rise to an uncovering.

Not so much, in a subjective or psychological way, because this reduction of presence would begin to infer a lack, to distil a regret (according to lyricism's old theme: retreat-regret) which, breaking satisfaction, would once again induce desire. Nor, in this illuminating withdrawal, is it any longer a question simply of the well-known virtue of the negative which, in contrast, gives a greater emphasis to it, or of the shadows of the painting that call attention to the colours. In fact, in this rupture of the springing up/settling, there appears and comes incidentally to thought nothing less than *non-coincidence* with itself, which due to this fact eludes the grip of logic (that of 'being' and of expression) through which life is in life and can be *effectively* experienced. In this way the moment of the withdrawal is instructive. The flight seems to exist but does not appear (only poetry, especially that which is modern and 'matinal', like that of Rimbaud or René Char, points towards it); the settling is obvious but, no longer being prominent, is not discerned (such is the case of the 'finished' painting, or of the stolen letter placed on the mantelpiece). But because the withdrawal de-prescribes (it is the 'being' of presence that prescribes), and already allows the penetration of the other into the 'self', as the latter therefore begins to disappropriate itself, cracking the fullness and cutting it away, in such a way that this fullness loses its opacity and can from that point play its full effect, only the withdrawal creates appearance, in other words, by (itself) withdrawing, it reveals the ground from which this springing up emerges.

This is now no longer the beginning of the afternoon but of the *evening*, when the light begins to withdraw and not only do things finally spring up anew under its oblique rays but also we discover in particular what (but which is not a 'what') is invisible but allows itself to win through the darkness while still resisting it and differentiating itself from it, making a virtue of the light. Similarly, the *autumn*—summer is withdrawing everywhere, settling down growth and carrying nature to its apex; it is not only the nostalgia of this completed plenitude and its radiance that is granted. 'What' appears, because it reappears from difference, 'what', but object–non-object, more fundamental than any description and of which the prior escapes, bearing that which we call too conveniently (synthetically) *nature* to this deployment. Banal themes they may be, the one as much as the other, whether we ordinarily confine them in a note or an aside, or make us soon topple over into bad lyricism. What they then deliver of this *effective* (from which, often very clumsily—because sentimentally—any *determining* statement already deviates and leads to failure) should not be neglected. Poetry is there (invents itself) in order to bring back to light what *logos* has lost (an impossible 'what').

Otherwise, we only begin to perceive 'what' living is when life is already withdrawing into ourselves, through old age or sickness, and not when it rises in power or spreads out in maturity. It is like Montaigne's variations around this impossible object in his last essay ('On Experience'): due to the fact that, from one day to the next, through respites and jerks, pauses and relapses, life is silently in the process of leaving him, he finally discerns and brings to consciousness this emotion from an earlier time of feeling everything but which the plenitude of life had earlier concealed—the emotion of simply existing in life (see also Rousseau in *Confessions* [2008] and the *Reveries* [2011]). Again, it is when I am about to leave you that I experience the strength of our relation—presence, as it is extended, is lost in it: not that I want to put it to the test, or that I count malignly on reviving it through its lack, but what is evident is sealed up and which presence obstructs; while the conclusion of a coming separation already decants presence which no longer conceals the relation of its opacity.

3

What then do we perceive that is disturbing, which already points into this divergence—of springing up and settling, or of the evidence and the withdrawal? Suppose this were nothing less than having to think of another form of coherency, provided we retrace this thread just a little—'coherence' here overflowing logic? The first, which believes it is alone, is obviate and triumphant (at least in the European *logos* as Aristotle regulated it). To what extent has it then, due to this very fact (because it does not confront itself), become conscious? A coherence by *coincidence*, which is properly 'logical', resting on the determination-definition and serving as a norm for the predicative statement—such is the logic of what is 'inherent', which assumes an identity that is justified in Being and which poses first of all the axiom of non-contradiction. It finds its subjective anchoring at the heart of classical philosophy in 'evidence', as the perfect presence of the thought object and as 'idea', thereby producing 'clarity' in the mind which perceives it and being illustrated in the traditional conception of truth as appropriateness and conformity—and upon which science is founded.

Would it not be suddenly to reveal itself as inadequate to think life as envisaged, not in its determination which fixes it but in what I just called its *effective* character that constantly dissociates it from itself? Since it is equally no longer 'being', it does not deliver itself into a 'what', without being a possible 'object'—'life'. Grasped from the disjunction of the springing up / settling, life begins making a hole in this appropriateness which reason has weaved so well and which claims to envelop everything in its tentacles—what Nietzsche called the *spider's web*. Indeed, once this hole is revealed, do we not see it widening into a breach, opposing one to the other? As soon as it makes the choice of knowledge (of essence, appropriateness, logic, truth . . .), philosophy has failed the phenomenon of life, of life as life, in other words, what ceaselessly passes into its other (or is otherwise death)? Or, rather, will we not suspiciously have to ask ourselves, so as to be able to think more conveniently (adequately) about its now petrified 'objects'—the comfort with which Nietzsche precisely reproached it—has it not turned away from life (has it not *fled* it)?

For how can we think of life except precisely as a continuous disappropriation of what is inherent to itself, therefore as what escapes itself without respite, which is its only possible definition, but is the same thing as its anti-definition, since it constantly passes into its other? Otherwise this adequacy kills life. Therefore is it as the *non-coincidence* of self with self—putting an end to the reign of the identity of a 'self'? Already the virtue which 'never leaves' virtue is consigned to being 'without virtue', effective ('superior') virtue having been withdrawn from it; or the 'beautiful' recognized as such is already a dead beautiful, that is, which is no longer effective, something from which the beautiful is in retreat. Or evidence, by saturating, is no longer distinguished, and only the withdrawal discloses. . . . But how can the coherence of this thought of non-coincidence be retained without allowing it to blur with mystery and holding it back from the abyss of Faith and its *absurdum*, God alone then outwitting logic as he pleases (from *Satz* as expressed to *Satz* as 'leap', as the German puts it so appropriately. See Heidegger 1939)? Or how to keep it from being tipped into paradox or provocation, which could last only for the period of a flash? How to avoid abandoning it to exoticism as to rhetorical play (the cult of the oxymoron) while it thereby challenges, as ostensibly as possible, the 'evidence' of logic?

But can we, first, separate from one another the evidence of things exhausted in the settling, as I have started to expose, and this subjective evidence as touchstone of truth, upon which rationalism relies, in such a sharp way? On the one hand, the external look is drowned in presence; on the other, a revenge which would then be assumed over the perceptible world, the gaze of the mind (for the mind would also be a 'gaze', a metaphor as old as metaphysics) finds its assurance, we are told, in the presence of the idea to the self. For all that, can we believe that this inherent ambivalence of evidence could be contained solely in this uncoupling of the intelligible and the physical?

Even intellectual 'evidence' can be a form of laziness—I see what appears to me to go without saying as evident in my mind, but it is perhaps what is so familiar to me that I have ceased to see what is arbitrary about it, about which I no longer have sufficient grasp to question myself. The coincidence, all coincidence, due to the very fact that there is coincidence, whether of the sight or the understanding, no longer leads to progress or work—this agreement is the threat of relaxation. The 'evidence', whatever it is, whether of the mind or perception, always runs the risk of this facility and renunciation. Just as that the evidence of things means that one no longer thinks about them, so the evidence of ideas means that one no longer sees them. When I say 'it is evident', I stop, lay down my weapons and cease to question. Let us ask ourselves: Does not this logical evidence, which we claim to go back to, in order to drive out all prejudice, hide a still greater prejudice? Is it not perched on some greater fundamental blindness?

A double programme, consequently, on two fronts or two sides. On the one hand, the condition and the laws of logical evidence are to be reconsidered in a still more exacting way, working to dispel obscurity, while some comfort is hidden in it in such a way that it could still serve as a point of unimpeachable (universal) pertinence of thought and that knowledge could gain a foothold over it, for want of being able to found itself in it. I do not want to renounce the evidence (of the coincidence) upon which reason is supported. On the other hand, this work is always ahead of us, something which its very challenge renders suspect—that of bringing to light another coherence, an alternative, a non-logical logic, that of the non-coincidence or impropriety which, eluding the determinative knowledge of *logos*, could legitimately (alongside the knowledge of objects and making its place 'to one side' of this object [non-object], in other words, with neither bad conscience nor useless bravado) enlighten the *effective* nature of life. For neither do I want this non-coincidence, characteristic of living, to be allowed to be enclosed in the ineffable, to abandon it to the cult of the irrational nor to mystical revenge. How then to articulate calmly the one with the other, because one as much as the other has full rights (the 'knowledge' of 'science' and the 'thought' of 'existence'), this very opposition having been tipped over into the abstract? Who does not sees that its terms are today frozen?

It will therefore be necessary to begin by giving full measure to this juxtaposition or to this 'to one side' (of the two regimes of coherence) of coincidence *or* of non-coincidence, *alias* those which are respectively illustrated in evidence and withdrawal. For is it not a question here of the very polarity of thought, or do we not think precisely of both, in this tension, the 'appropriate' and its subversion? Is it not even this rival exigency which brings us to thought—brings thought to the forefront? Again, it is necessary to investigate with rigour what such a coexistence implies once one does not allow the absorption of what has begun at this point to make an unforeseeable 'hole' in rationality, in the shape of the 'withdrawal', at the heart of the great separation of territories, framed in advance, of the religious confronted with science.

Or, someone will object, would one not already find this coexistence allowed, and even, for want of being legalized, somewhat arbitrated, at the very heart of philosophy? For Descartes to perceive in his *cogito* the point at which the evidence emerges from which everything finally begins—for him to establish it thus as a principle of philosophy, uprooting doubt and constructing science on it; indeed, for him to make it the first rule of his method, the idea then 'presented' in such a clear way to the mind, because it occurs immediately, and for this coincidence, having become complete, to serve as the very foundation of truth—all this, as we know, will not prevent him from thinking about the 'use of the passions' (in the *Passions of the Soul* [1989], his great culminating work); indeed, to place within it alone 'all the sweetness and bliss of this life' as he confides to us in an aside (in a letter to the Marquis of Newcastle, March or April 1648), 'conceals' it. . . .

For all that, let us mark out in advance the fact that whether Descartes thought so long about the passions, taking a delight in distinguishing their variety, seeing in them what forms the charm and intensity of life; or whether, equally, before as after him, we have never ceased to think of the 'appetite' as the essence of man, or the power to be of the *conatus* (or the *Trieb* or the drive) as the very expression of life (indeed, whether, like Spinoza, God is conceived as life itself, or Being as the Will to power, into which Nietzsche unfortunately lapsed), it has never taken us an inch beyond the logic of the inherent and its pertinence. Even if one thinks of the impetuosity and the overflowing of life, life is still envisaged as a certain 'essence', and this does not at all contradict or even dissociate itself (or *de-coincide*) one little bit from itself—life does not always move in its concept, and no passage from a 'self' into the other is involved. Whether he therefore considers the contrariety of the soul or of the body or seeks the opposite, through some cerebral gland or animal spirits, a point of meditation or transition between them, Descartes never comes to suspect the principle of identity but always proceeds to confirm it—he does not allow life to disturb his thinking, to upset just a little the method of knowledge.

4

These two major options will thus decide between themselves, under the figures of *evidence* and *withdrawal*, and their standing one against the other remains to be constructed—*bicephalous* is philosophy, doubling confronted: the coherences of coincidence *or* of non-coincidence, the logic of the 'inherent' and 'non-inherent' (regimes of *homo-* or *hetero-*logy). There remains the identification of the object/subject or the thinking of life. Who does not see that, along this demarcation line, phenomenology itself is detached from rather than promoting the conditions of coexistence? Between the principle of *evidence* to which one returns again and again (Husserl) as the only conceivable starting point from which to constitute the possibility of science, and the meditation of the *withdrawal* by which alone Being can be thought (Heidegger), in carrying it to the point of dissociation of itself from itself as 'being'. Does phenomenology emerge from what it experiences in this way less as a fertile tension than as a rupture and an alternative (*Evidenz/Entzug*)? For it has let itself be spellbound

either by one or by the other—either by what undeniably springs into the mind's eye and from which it
can firmly begin in order to establish knowledge, or
by the appeal to rise ever higher, to the dispossessing,
groundless grounds, of the truth—and this to the
point that such a truth could finally renounce itself as
truth.

For, whether the 'evidence' would be not simply
the point of departure but also the sole unshakeable
justification of science, or whether it would really be
the only way of having the thing present to consciousness, and not just as presumed or what is aimed at, or
whether it therefore corresponds to the complete covering of one by the other, the gaze of the mind then
reaching the 'thing itself' and already doing so in
the ante-predicative state (by virtue of 'primitive evidence'), such is really the coincidence from which, in
the footsteps of Descartes (in *Cartesian Meditations*
[Husserl 1977]), subjectivity (grasping itself then
as 'pure' or 'transcendental' self) can always be made
to emerge and at the least cost. Likewise, before
Descartes, it was not a question, properly speaking,
of evidence but of clarity which would of necessity
be logical (the *delon oti* of the Greeks). It was upon
this, the 'living' evidence of the 'I am', that Husserl
founded the ('indisputable') absolute of knowledge.

Yet, from the point of view considered here, the question remains and I am not making any progress. For how can this 'living', seized solely in the intuition of a moment, extend to the point of being able to account for the *effective* of life, in other words, of life envisaged in its course and passing into its other, by which life is life, a disappropriation of the inherent, and eluding itself?

'Evident' means, in short, the height of the 'inherent', a limit on this side to which one could not go back—not any longer by virtue of the axiom posed (as in Aristotle) but (from Descartes to Husserl) of a subjectively experienced presence. How then to be sure of being able to block this, completely isolatable, presence in its mind? This is what is responded to in an exemplary way by disclosing this 'inherent' (Heidegger in *Was ist Metaphysik?* [1998], where the rupture is seen for the first time): if it is true that science itself, in its 'inherent' determination, is interested only in being itself (and does not want to know anything about 'nothing'), by the same token it finds itself dependent on this 'nothing' from which it turns aside and yet is committed to, which is therefore necessarily postponed, as it decides itself, from prior to itself. From this it appears that even science *does not coincide* with itself (that it is *zwiespältig*) and cannot close in upon itself (the 'being') except by equally overflowing from it—the ground is therefore never the ground but opens onto an unfathomable (*Abgrund*) 'without ground' in which the Cartesian tree of philosophy takes root without dreaming about it. It will therefore be impossible to fix a radical point of departure; so one is obliged to rise still higher towards the original—towards precisely that point at which, while eluding the understanding, the oppositions effectively coincide: where, by the fact that we relegate the nothingness, we still allege it and thereby it is Being itself which at once, contradictorily, 'exposes and conceals itself'—'agrees and slips away': where Being cannot therefore reveal itself, in the settling of being, except in 'withdrawing' as Being and so on.

What will we be able to gain, from this other (Heideggerian) side, to think about 'living'? And what will we be able to learn about this figure of 'withdrawal', breaking with the prestige of evidence and exploring it in 'Being'? If Being is primarily thought about, we recall, as a coming to presence, and this by opposition to the (fixed) present-duration of the being of the metaphysic, we are now drawn to consider, taking a step further but in a backwards, not capital, way, that it is only the 'withdrawal' of Being but a withdrawal that is 'hidden' and which allows this emergence of the present as 'being'. In other words, and making this original dependency better understood in relation to an Other and such that it discloses all thought of the inherent or of coincidence—it is only from a withdrawal that presence exists as it is; or, presence is no longer thought simply in its difference with the present but insofar as it is more originally its contrary: the 'withdrawal'. Thus the 'inherent property' (the coincidence) is itself disappropriated in its ground and always requires us to return to what came earlier.

Is this not, in fact, what was already thought, as Heidegger tells us, in this first word by which the Greeks conceived of the coming of existence, or the entrance into presence, the *phusis*, in its first rising and its 'drive', but that had then been defined *too neatly*— flatly (by 'settling' I would say)—as 'nature'? For, if this is conceived as a constant 'giving birth', an emergence and rising of the (to the) appearance (*Aufgehen*), in other words, as the *springing up*, we also know, according to the famous formulation of Heraclitus, that it 'loves to hide' and finds in this occultation, which constitutes its reserve, that which alone guarantees its surge. The same goes for what is also called in such an inherent and therefore undeserved way *truth*. If the Greeks conceived it as an 'unveiling' (*aletheia, Unverborgenheit*), it was (a thesis now familiar to the point of cliché) because it refers more essentially to a 'veiling' (*lethé*) which not only constitutes its fundamentals (*fonds*), the reserve or the condition, but also, through its contrary dimension, governs it continuously from within. And which, by withdrawing to the benefit of the unveiling, in this way equally dispenses itself in it.

5

What is there in this that can be retained (levied from this dissociation of 'Being' from 'being', of the withdrawal of Being allowing the deployment of being, or of the 'veiling' and its 'unveiling') that will here clarify the disjunction between the *springing up* and its *settling*? Consequently, what could serve to account for the impropriety, or *non-coincidence*, which makes life and its renewal *effective*? At least, by default, coincidence, unable to allow itself to be blocked in presence, having sealed the 'evidence', could no longer be the unshakeable point of departure and, as such, the 'founder' of science. For it always opens on this side of itself onto its contrary, by which it escapes—on a more essential non-coincidence in whose name it now has to be concluded that, science, because it does not depart from the thought of the 'inherent property' that, according to the well-known phrase, 'doesn't think'. From that point a conclusion can no longer close over it, to coincide with the self; we are sent back to a point upstream upon which it depends (but which has withdrawn from it to let it be, and this to the point of making it 'forget' it) and the fundamental impropriety of every statement (recounting the 'proper') is proved. Of this disclosure in its ground, abyssal and even vertiginous, the moment of coincidence, afterwards, in the settled no longer appears as anything more than an outcrop, isolatable by the fact of this very withdrawal and such that has been fixed by 'logic'.

But in this properly interminable dispossession, does this *dispropriation* commit us? Is it not too costly? Because as soon as we disclose each determination in its fundamentals to go back to that upon which it depends, which at the same time has withdrawn from it and illuminates it, so that we concede that nothing more remains in the self, or that the 'inherent property' is not a 'self' but that from which the latter proceeds, therefore that its presence is each time de-circumscribed in order to enquire into its provenance, then we shall find no further reason to put a stop to this step back: to seek a ground within the ground, to go back into this opening—to retrocede towards the increase of light which at the same time projects greater obscurity. There no longer remains any 'evidence' (of isolatable presence or 'inherent property') on which to settle comfortably. Or if we finally stop at a 'first' conclusion, considered to be the most original (the totally undetermined 'it', of an initial 'there is', *es gibt*), this inevitably means nothing more—it can only serve to name the impossible property at the heart of any statement.

If Heidegger is so often compelled to justify the fact that the 'inherent' should be thought of as order, not essence, but from the upstream, not of the ground but of the non-ground, and for that reason to pass from 'representation' to 'comprehension' (*vorstellen/ verstehen*) and get rid of the too narrowly, because isolating, correct way of thinking about understanding; indeed, that it calls for the dissolution of 'the very idea of logic' in the 'vortex of a more original investigation', this is what can serve momentarily to mark out the way by integrating the contradiction and legitimating it, through various expedients, but which for all that will not suffice. I have skirted his thought for a while, but must here leave it. To think of the dis-propriation proper to *living* and leading it to break with the identity ordinarily imposed on the concept, in other words, to draw more into the light the de-coincidence inherent to this concept—non-concept Heidegger leaves us stuck on at least two points.

First, I cannot see that Heidegger illuminated the relation of this most essential non-coincidence with respect to the logic (of the inherent or coincidence) from which it detaches itself—he did not make explicit what coherence it was a question of in regard to the other, that on which knowledge is built, needing therefore to justify them both at the same time and maintaining them in parallel. At the risk otherwise of being driven to abandon science, the status of the object as well as technology, as also the construction of politics—issues upon which, as we know, his thought stumbles—and to need to make a secret return to the *quia absurdum* of theology, to which we see him constrained, even once more to call upon the resources of apophatic thought. Likewise, he was unable to illuminate how thought needs not to renounce the inherent property (of knowledge) but actively to evolve from one to the other—from the inherent to the non-inherent and back again—and work in the *divergence* which provokes it: between coincidence and non- (or rather de-)coincidence, *between* the immediate seizing of evidence, furnishing the clarity of a possible grasp and support, something as such indispensable for the work of thought *and* the penetrating (the deepening) into the without-ground of the withdrawal.

Further, by withdrawing into the 'Question of Being', does Heidegger not in the end forsake the existential analysis by whose guiding thread, however, he had first thought to gain access to Being (such as, in *Sein und Zeit*, the analysis of anguish)? By focusing only on the ontological quest, in this way extending and reducing all de-coincidence simply into the relation of Being and being and to the advantage of Being alone, he can only, in consequence, once more and in spite of the denials of usage, fall into the facilities of retrocession and hypostasis; and, in doing so, without warning, philosophy has once more *given up on life*.

This thought crosses over, in fact, but once again still leaves us in the dark, even if only for those couple of moments that alerted us, alternating the one with the other, as much from the settling as from the withdrawal—from the withdrawal from the springing up at the heart of what is settled as well as from what the withdrawal of what is settled reveals but which this settling of evidence no longer allowed to be discerned. Admittedly, it approaches, but does not give a better or definitive account of what the *Laozi*, without making it explicit, brought out and that of which it is the index remains to be followed further—simply, that is, phenomenologically and without superimposing anything onto it (without crushing it), that, from the virtue which coincides with its tangible marks and that could be defined, even though an inferior and curtailed virtue, as 'superior', the previous virtue has already withdrawn from it, to the point that what is currently called *virtue* is no longer effective virtue but a fallen and codified virtue. How then to be satisfied with this elementary or *simple*, on a level with experience, that of the 'living' or of the 'effective', without allowing it to be hidden by the ontological apparatus? How not to slip from it?

For the effectivization to be withdrawn from what is effective in it does not for all that imply that this 'what' can be substantialized—in which respect ontology is definitively misleading. In this respect, all thought that is retroceded in 'Being' in order to reside there (such 'hiding' constituting the essence of Being, as Heidegger says, and so on) is effectively without an exit. Likewise, even though Heidegger reproaches Husserl precisely with not having understood this appeal to return 'to things themselves' (*zur Sache selbst*), an appeal that philosophy has endlessly been reviving from one age to the next, in echo and with perseverance, at least since the time of Aristotle, did not Heidegger himself, along the way, equally betray it without realizing that he had done so? At the risk, which we can see only too well, of enclosing its reflection in terms that are increasingly taken out of any sort of experience, or which leave existence to be played out, and of having to fall back on just the resource of the internal play inherent to language and its etymology—to find itself, in sum, in service to its only tool, with no more grain to grind, this want of mastery no longer compensating itself (would one risk saying so?) except by prophesy. In truth, did Heidegger perceive/conceive of the 'withdrawal' *phenomenologically* (not metaphysically)?

As proof: the way in which Heidegger gives an account, definitively, of the phenomenon of the 'lighting' or 'clearing', *Lichtung* (1976), which is such a well-known theme. The clearing in the trees, he tells us, is experienced by contrast with the dense thickness of the forest (*Dickung*)—it is a 'clearing', to speak precisely, rather than a 'glade' (even if this is the sanctified translation), since it is a question here not of an absence of trees in a given and circumscribed place but of a rarefaction crossing the forest through and through—the woodcutters speak of making a clearing in a mature forest in order to help the trees to grow better. For it is a question not of suppressing but of pruning, of simply making the meshing less tight—not of stripping but of spacing out. The reclamation is not total but, through the withdrawal it puts into effect, the perspectives are once more opened up. In fact, Heidegger reminds us that 'clearing' means, due to its adjective, 'to render lighter' (*etwas lichten*) and therefore, he insists, has nothing in common 'either in language or as to the thing', with the semanticism of *licht* meaning 'clear' or 'luminous'. Heidegger then suddenly retrocedes (but why does he suddenly break with the logic of the image?) that 'nevertheless' (*gleichwohl*) the possibility still being maintained 'from a connection of fact between the two', the light, *Licht*, can 'effectively' (*nämlich*) visit the *Lichtung* ('fall into it': *einfallen*), which can only then render possible the coming of light as it spreads into this opening.

Why suddenly this about-turn, and to what does it therefore effectively constitute the concession? Why not be satisfied with the fact that the clearing alone operates—that it is the *withdrawal* (of the trees) which lights up *of itself*? For, by desaturating and dis-encumbering, in rendering the trees 'light-sown', thinned-out, this withdrawal alone suffices to make apparent. The trees stand out better due simply to the fact that, having been extricated, they enter once more into tension with one another, distinguishing them-selves and effecting a dynamic exchange (as Chinese painting has learnt so well to render in representing them under the brush). Letting in absence through the presence, filtering out the void rather than the light, but not allowing it to settle—this withdrawal effectively allows the remaining plenitude, by being emptied away, to complete its full effect. Is not such a clearing also experienced in the half-light? For it is disappearance that is the condition of appearance, since presence cannot illuminate of itself but obstructs; this is what makes the withdrawal necessary. But why then *in addition* invoke the light (as Heidegger did)? Why make the 'clearing' a particular territory (a privileged site) in whose clarity alone everything that 'exists' can appear? Why not be satisfied with the virtue of the pruning but want the light to *come* and inundate? The pruning in itself is lighting. The ray of light (*Lichtstrahl*) is not what imports the light which is what is born from the lightening, by rarefaction, of what is opaque. Otherwise, there is the risk of having to fall back *in fine* into the old metaphysical setting, as Heidegger does here, in which the Light comes to illuminate the 'idea' of which we nevertheless blithely believed we had rid ourselves.

6

In thinking through the withdrawal, I have until now been careful to keep away from religion. But the ground constantly slips towards it, towards its abyss—in the European context, the Withdrawal of itself inclines towards it. By yielding up his Son, God withdrew. He disappropriates from Himself to become appropriated in a man who came to save humans—a great *muthos* illuminating life. In considering the withdrawal of the initial 'it' (of the donor 'there is', *es gibt*), can Heidegger not help disclosing that he is inspired by it? For it is in the Christian figure of God that, in the West, the fundamental inappropriateness or the non-coincidence of self with self, by which the concept of life can alone be animated, is thought most radically and by which alone the concept of life itself is able to *live*, whereas the coincidence with self, enclosing and stabilizing it in the self, turns it into an inert 'self' (from which alone life, all in all, triumphing from the identity of essence which would fix it in itself, can find its concept). God sent his son (He the Father) claiming to be a slave (He the Master), sees Himself dying (He the Eternal). It is necessary for God to depart and renounce his self, pass into his other and go as far as to experience the contrary of the self in order to become the 'living God' (as 'Spirit').

If God is declared to be 'living', it is not therefore so much that God should come to earth and live among people; nor that His Son could serve as a mediator showing the way towards Him; nor even that, in being resurrected, He triumphs from the death of the man. It is, rather, because, through his Son, 'God' is opposed in an exemplary way to Himself, and this occurs within Himself; disappropriating Himself of self and escaping self, instead of remaining (mortally) within the self—something which is really, among all monotheisms, the original idea of Christianity. Therefore this is the way in which Christianity is that fertile thought which carried it, through its Greek message, scandalously to confront philosophy and, because of this, to compensate it (the brilliant intuition of Paul raising the 'madness' of the cross to face the *sophia* of the world) and so make the evangelical message the other of philosophy. Its effect was to raise religion at a stroke to the level of philosophy and to disclose what the latter lacks, therefore already reversing it. Such a denunciating opposition serves for each to fill in for what has become the glaring defect of the other—faced with the dismal identity (the impassibility) of the essences posed by philosophy, the dramatization which holds life in tension is revealed; or, faced with the 'inherent properties' upon which knowledge is built, the fundamental error which causes life to be called upon to break away from itself in order to redefine itself in its other without ceasing to be alive is made clear. Saint John already knew how to locate this inexhaustible vein, and to unravel this promising thread (12:25): 'What is attached to life loses its life'; or that it is necessary to renounce life in order to be able to deploy life (eternally).

This was the point at which, as the Greeks had decided—we had now started to think in terms of essence or the 'inherent' instead of the difference and dehiscence inherent to life except by challenging the inherent or depropriation—there remained no other resource, in the theoretical context, that is, that of Europe and facing this regime of determination-definition of what is inherent, to which the *logos* constrains us than openly to introduce the rupture and return to the fiction-function of the narrative, *muthos*, within it. Faced with the discourse of knowledge, perched on non-contradiction, no other path remains, in short, to think about life, than to conceive of this other discourse, but it is a discourse–non-discourse: the Word demanding contradiction even in God (Christ is entirely a man and a God at the same time); as well as making depropriation the very essence of life: God dying as a slave on the cross. For to limit the existence of things to their definition, as science teaches, to confine them in their determinations or properties, in short, to hold them completely coincident with themselves, pinning them down in themselves, means that life is able to escape from these things themselves: the *episteme*, 'science' as Aristotle already said, would be from the same root as *stenai*, to stop. Therefore, let us once again unbind the religious from its casing or its bark—such an old allegorizing gesture of philosophy: this religious in Europe has not so much aimed to maintain the hope of a beyond and teach about final ends, or at least this was not what made it a logically necessity. More crucially, it has served to point the finger towards that other truth, but a truth this time by fundamental inadequacy which, as consciousness of life and finding itself repressed by the rationality of science, could no longer burst in except on its opposite—the Mystery. Unable to institute a counter-logic, of non-coincidence or non-inherence, directly, there was no choice than to consecrate it in 'God'. Philosophers ('theosophers'), on the German side of philosophy, who came more or less clandestinely to draw from this source in turn, refused the great, very convenient, separation of reason and faith, *alias* of science and religion, on which classical thought rested until the very middle of the reign of the Enlightenment. They wanted to illuminate the phenomenon of life in its own coherence (although an illogical coherence): from Eckhart to Boehme ('Grasp the no in the yes and the yes in the no,' said Boehme); or from Boehme to Hegel ('think the pure life, that is the task,' Hegel confided in his youthful writings); or from Hegel to Heidegger, taking from Hegel the (romantic) idea of a science which, contrary to its Cartesian-Husserlian definition, works to overcome the finite in order to reach 'infinite knowledge' which alone is capable of 'effectively' containing life in its concept.

A note by Jean Hyppolite in his great *Genesis and Structure of Hegel's 'Phenomenology of Spirit'* (1974) signals this in passing: a certain interpretation of Christianity, 'according to which it was only through becoming a man and knowing death and human destiny so as to surmount them that God became God ... is implicit in Hegelianism'. One would then like, in the great Hegelian pin cushion, to see this thread which disturbs drawn anew—would it not moreover provide its guiding thread? One would like to see this undeniable but awkward idea developed (overall Hegel, in the development of his thought, only thought to give a logical form to this initial irrationality to which his thinking of life confronted him)—in other words, so as to think through the concept of life, finally to enter life in the concept (in Hegelian terms, to elevate it so it becomes an 'absolute concept'). For if he did retain the dramatic (Christian) image of an Absolute which splits itself and tears itself in order to be absolute as a backdrop, this internal difference would remain fully qualitative, hence his rupture with Schelling. Hegel no less worked, with all his strength, to integrate (absorb) it through philosophy; and the greater the effort to get to the end of the resistance, the more fertile is thought.

On this very long path of consciousness, in fact, after he had already considered the contradictory nature of 'strength', at once positive and negative, in this way causing the 'thingism' of the 'perception' (*Wahrnehmung*) of the true to emerge, therefore of a logic of representation content to isolate and juxtapose properties, at what did Hegel arrive (at the most intense moment of *Phenomenology*, see Hegel 1977: Chapter 4), if not this new certitude, finally rising to the consciousness of self: That the property of each determination is really, in a general way, to reveal the contrary of itself? That it is therefore necessary tirelessly to emerge from determinations constituted from their closure and fixity in order to allow their internal movement and their 'fluidity' (*Flüssigkeit*) or, as Hegel again says, their 'anxiety', to appear. For the 'self' could never coincide fully with the self (that is, to be 'equal' to self, otherwise it would be a dead 'self'), but would be conducted to pass into its other in order to be itself, consequently constantly to contradict itself within itself and making this negation of self its only possible identity, such is really the only property of a living 'self', finally promoted into sub-ject and no longer being sub-stance: a 'subject' which, instead of letting it reify itself into its identity (as Descartes does with the *res cogitans*), might reach within itself to the 'process' of life, a henceforth rival term that Hegel, here, crosses with the other—*das Leben als Prozess*.

But we also know how Hegel betrayed this intuition of life through the dialectic—by introducing into it the finality of a going beyond, which absorbed the contradiction as it surmounted it, and therefore returning from it to the thought of a final coincidence (absolute Knowledge) which would conclude all process. Hegel approached the concept of life (that is, its own de-coinciding and depropriating content) but could not be satisfied with it; he toppled back *in fine* into pertinence *through* agreement and inherent nature (*propriété*), *alias* classical truth. Long and painful as the Hegelian development of the Spirit would therefore be, pursued mercilessly from stage to stage, obliged at each to abandon the preceding certainty, it is on the whole merely temporary—in the image of poverty of man on earth—and Reconciliation-appropriateness awaits. It is therefore no doubt the case that a thought of non-coincidence, in Europe, is always heroic, and grasped at the last moment. It always stems from vertigo and in the face of the reign of *logos*, that of the determination-definition, finds support only in dramatization and religious eschatology, remains marked by a lack and an irrationality—struck by an 'absurdity' that can only save the mystery of the *absurdum*. Consequently, it likewise remains bewitching and tempting. Here, therefore, is what once more drives the return to the question of departure: Does the thought of non-coincidence allowing life to be thought about exclude all coherence as it emerges from logic? Or, as the vice is loosened, how can a passage be found between the two? Between what pours out into the abyss of mystery and the conversion, and what brings a return to the logic of what is inherent, betraying life once more?

7

This would imply once again a return to our cultural prejudices in order to undo the bolts which, without our knowledge, have perhaps been allowed to lock up our thought. This needs to be done in order to give back intelligence, all intelligence, its freedom to manoeuvre and allow it a fresh initiative: Could we set out from higher up as a beginning? In this respect, travelling (by thought) is not exotic but *ex-optic*. The interest in calling once again upon China is (do I need to say it again?) to perceive the question from another angle—to discover it on a fresh day, finally drawing it out of the atavistic framework which in Europe it has made its own, and in which its destiny is found somewhat sealed up, no matter how inventive the effort of philosophy to free itself from it may consequently be. Like all activity, thought also *gets bogged down*, as does life. Chinese thought, we note, not being focused on the determination-definition of the inherent, to which the Greek *logos* is devoted, which founds its rigour, nor having any of the religious setting of a grand Narrative with its dramatic knotting and unknotting, sees in this a delicate and 'subtle' point which needs to be tackled with a 'subtle' intelligence and by taking the opposite path to that of common opinion. But for all that does it create a problem, some challenge cast at reason?

After having stated that 'superior' and eminent virtue is hollow 'like a vale', for it appears deficient (or, according to the preceding formulae, familiarizing us with this statement: that 'the path which advances appears to be stepping back', 'the flat path appears to be indented', etc.), the *Laozi* does not suffer from a longing to establish the non-coincidence that would allow life to be thought about: 'The large square, when finally allowed to fall, has no corners' (§41). This formula places us more than as openly as possible in rupture with the logic of *logos*. But does it make an appeal to mystery? In the same way that 'virtue' which 'remains within virtue' is 'without virtue', the square which does not leave its determination as a square, which is enclosed in its definition as a square ('square-square'), is revealed to be cramped up, having become sterile, and no longer deploys its 'extent' or 'greatness' as a square. In fact, what does 'great' mean here? Not that it would be a question of stature, obviously (on that basis, the *tao* can equally well be declared 'small'), but this description put forward: 'square', instead of folding up on its determination, of enclosing itself in its appropriateness, maintains itself in its deployment, in *flight*; in a de-determination which keeps it from sticking to its definition as a 'square' and *spreads out* from it.

Therefore 'Great' here means whatever does not allow itself to be riveted to its determination but, divesting itself of its ground, prevents itself from being immobilized and fixed; from settling down in an essence subject to knowledge (which is where, consequently, the Taoist teaching of 'inscience', from which alone one can grasp life, originates). When it is comes to characterizing the *dao*, the 'way', the *Laozi* can, in fact, only, 'in forcing', it says, call it *great*; but this denomination, far from being constituted as a stable attribute, is immediately abandoned as soon as it is proposed. Hardly has it been stated than it is terminated—the formulation is in continuous transformation:

> *In forcing, I call it great,*
> *great is called (means) leaving,*
> *leaving is called (means) distanced,*
> *distanced is called (means) returning (§25).*

We can see how, in a concerted way, going from one term to another, the statement eludes itself, dispossessing itself of one to assume possession of the other, revealing in this way an inappropriateness which is not for all that a flaw (referring to the well-known ineffable) but the very process of the 'way' (of life) by which, constantly de-coinciding with itself, it continually advances and renews itself. Instead of resting in each proposed term, this statement in effect systematically detaches itself from itself and is carried off course. Each of these terms therefore serves no longer precisely as a 'terminus', demarcating and 'terminating' meaning, but as a stage. Not that, precisely speaking, the next term goes beyond the one that came before, or even says anything more about it, but retrieving what the latter lost, by isolating and demarcating meaning, it saves it from the determination into which it became bogged down.

We will therefore understand that, breaking with a whole tradition of translation (correction), I am not be tempted to amend this formula from the *Laozi* (immediately following up the 'great square has no corner[s]'): 'The great work avoids happening'; and that, without fear of such a radicality of meaning, I do not hastily adopt what is, once reversed, simply a weakened version of it, but renew it with the expected common sense of logic: 'The great work is accomplished this evening' (*wan*, with the key addition of the sun, being substituted for *mian*, 'to avoid'[3]). Not only is this *lectio facilior* desperately flat, defusing in advance everything which would promote thought, but it also makes a hole in what follows of these stated forms; while the best-established lesson, that which I am, integrating perfectly in this development, sends us back as appropriately as possible to what we already know about the sketch and illuminates it— the work is affirmed all the better as work (remaining *effective*) when it prevents itself from sinking into a complete determination; that, remaining upstream from a definitive actualization, it preserves, at the very heart of its figuration, these fundamentals from which it is painted and from where its surge arises—in other words, what maintains it alive. Holding itself withdrawn from any of the effects of settling, it thereby avoids immobilizing itself into a certain form, one that is completed and rests in its identity, fixing it in its particularity. In this way, the 'great image' prevails in it, as is said in what follows (which uses the same meaning of 'great'): 'The great image has no form ...'

Neither, consequently, should we be surprised that Chinese thought could perceive the 'way', *dao*, other than under the form of the Withdrawal. But it is a 'withdrawal' which is precisely paired with its 'deployment'—the way needs to withdraw in order to allow it still to occur. The relation between the two is expressed without surprise by an 'empty' word', in Chinese (*er*), meaning at once concession and consequence ('but / so that'): while they are opposed, the one is the condition of the other. Only the withdrawal allows deployment; or the disappearance is the condition of the appearance. Then, far from making it a statement that contravenes reason, the conquest of the high struggle at the price of a desperate retrocession,

Chinese thought presents it as self-evident, taking all schools together—we see its *ground of understanding* there. Already on the Confucian incline, it is said of the Sage: 'The way of the Sage dispenses (spends itself) at the same time as it withdraws' ('conceals': *fei er yin*—*Zhong yong*, §12); or 'withdraws' at the same time as it 'appears' (*yin er xian, Liji, 'Biaoji'*): it is both expansive and slips away (*sich bekundet und verbirgt, gewährt und entzieht*, said Heidegger for his part, as though he was translating.[4]). The way already spreads out to the point of 'simple couples', the classical Chinese says, but, in its intimate ground, it eludes even the Sage.

The fact that the great square has no corner(s), or the great work avoids happening, or that the great image has no form, leads the *Laozi* to conclude in the same way about the Withdrawal:

The way withdraws: nameless,
only the way is fitted to grant and make happen
(§41, end).

The way, the *dao*, withdraws or hides (*yin*), to the point that it is no longer nameable, but this is what allows it to constantly spread and dispense. Heidegger again: 'Being is destined for us, but in such a way that it withdraws at the same time into its essence'

(1957a: 122). The 'there' of the original 'there is', says Heidegger, the final term of the retrocession (of the *Ereignis*, as 'to occur inherently', as untranslatable a word, he tells us, as the Greek *logos* or the Chinese *tao*), is absolutely nothing outside the function which belongs to it but it is what everything must return to. Just as the 'way' *dao* is not at all a supreme concept, *Oberbegriff* (Heidegger 1998: 22), so also it does not designate any specific entity—it signifies only that it is the withdrawal which allows to 'make happen' and to 'accord' (*shan dai qie cheng*).

What does it definitively bring to the intelligence of this coherence, not to call it *Being*, or not to call it minimally *It*, *es*, but the 'way', *dao*? No doubt that, the withdrawal *not being at all assignable*, it is the dispensation which is also a withdrawal—without there therefore being anything metaphysical to unmake and without there being anything, in Chinese, to force the language somewhat: the formula flows from the source. It is no longer a play upon paradox; it takes the opposite view to that of facile thought but 'establishes itself' (*jian yan*) without challenging. There would not be anything there to construct thought, however little— thought hardly takes off. Is another revelation to be expected? But it is already the case that, every year, fertility withdraws into the earth to bloom when a new spring comes—*phusis*; or that all effectivity withdraws from its effectivization, to the extent that it is settled, in order to remain effective in it. Or, when, in plain view, the painter keeps his sketch incomplete, the work withdraws into its invisible fundamentals to let the latter appear. It is no longer the determined and definable, coinciding, life, but that from which life *is alive*, from which life wells up, de-coinciding with itself to remain in flight, that, from this simple action, by staying its hand, it illuminates.

III

THE ENTRANCE OF LIFE

1

What awareness of 'living' can we assume from within when it is what 'constitutes' us from the outset, without any possible exteriority? What could be most anchored (just the biological) and least already oriented (according to ideological choices)? We may say 'what', but this 'what' is not local; we may say 'from the outset', but for each of us this very beginning escapes us. Of this too-representative 'what' within which we find ourselves forever immerged and from which we can never distance ourselves, therefore, without sufficient conditions of reflexivity, let us extricate at least some basic, obviate, assertion from 'life' on which to alight—which would not tip us over immediately into the interpreted. Instead of straddling this triviality, which is too vulgar for us to pause over, let us count upon this greater radicality, let uss start off at the level of experience—life is hunger; life is thirst.

What is the initial difference to be made between what is in life and what is not in life? Everything that is not in life *coincides* with itself, without any inverse internal tension within itself—this hollowness is simply hollow; it can hollow itself out further, to the point of being entirely emptied. But life (what makes life) is this hollow of hunger, as it hollows itself out, demanding to be filled: this minus is no longer simply a minus but a *lack*—life is what is constantly being worked upon by what is opposed to it. Plato poses this in the most general way: the *business* of all living (*epicheiresis*), what constitutes its constant effort, is that it 'leads in a direction that is opposite to what it experiences' (*Philebus*: 35c). Life, in other words, is grasped in this 'between'—between the state which affirms itself, and the opposed state to which it aspires. It has been emptied but is calling to be filled; it is a cask that leaks what is constantly being poured into it is, as Socrates said, such is the paradoxical image of its capacity.

Or, rather, Socrates proposes, let's compare life to two casks (*Gorgias*: 492–4). Would we allow our life to be nothing but a leaky cask, always slipping away, and into which our hungers and thirsts, and from them all our passions as soon as they are insatiable, would continually force us (although in vain) to pour? This would be like trying to fill such a cask with a sieve, insofar as our desires, being unlimited, from the outset would then let satisfaction elude what it strives for. Even before being able of hoping for some gratification, any fulfilment is, from the beginning, impossible. In order for our desires to know how to limit themselves, is it not necessary to make life into a cask which does not leak but into one which is well made, so that our desires know how to limit themselves—a cask which we can definitively fill up, without having constantly to keep pouring into it, thereby allowing us to rest without having to worry about it? Once the wise man, with his casks full, as Socrates shows, has mastered his desires and contained his hunger, demanding nothing more, he can live in peace.

But the man with casks brim-full, who no longer has to pour into them, is a dead man, replies Callicles without hesitation—finally *coinciding* with himself, without further divergence from self to self, without further tension projecting him outside his self, he lives as does a 'stone'. No longer having to 'pour', he no longer needs to live, 'no longer knowing either joy or sorrow', since sorrows are also legitimately part of life;

serving to activate it, he has wasted away. On the contrary, it is the endless quality of our hunger, the insatiability of our desires, the fact that we are never able to gratify ourselves and that our satisfactions always entail fresh deficiencies—that is a characteristic of life; in short, the cask should be leaky, so that there is a continual need to pour into it without it ever being possible to fill it up: more than this—this constitutes the charm of life. The characteristic of life (the charm of life) lies in the fact that we are still able 'to pour' (*epirrean*). 'No' (the bold 'no' which forever defies the conventions of morality): pouring without ever filling up forces us to work day and night, keeps us tied to the pressure of desire and prevents us from knowing rest; it is not to be escaped. Therefore, by renouncing the snare of contented satisfaction, Callicles says, we see in the everlasting renewal of lack not the punishment of the Danaides but the very condition of being alive; in other words, its resource, therefore as contented as life is.

Let us, therefore, not give in to the mirage of the coveted conclusion, the realization of what is hoped for, the arrival. Let us, says Callicles, challenge this facility of wisdom—and its laziness—according to which it would be better to live without any hunger, without lacking any thing—living without desire.

Such fulfilment of satisfaction does not leave anything beyond—gratified, one no longer lives. Let us even dare to propose this liberating reversal: in 'obtaining' we are not gaining anything, as we believe, but *losing the lack*. Of course, it would be worthless to denounce the futility of always having to pour. What is the point of pouring if one is never able to retain? Life may no longer be that of the 'stone', Socrates mocks, but of the 'plover' (the bird which is supposed continually to excrete what it is in the process of absorbing). And yet, the fact that we always have a fresh hunger, that our desires are never satisfied, rather than rendering life ridiculous is what keeps it progressing and active and maintains its vitality; it is what keeps it in tension in the *between*—between desire and satiety. It is precisely in this *between* that we live. Rather than dreaming of some ideal, terminal-optimal, state to which we would finally gain access so as to remain there forever, life is justified only as a lack whose satisfaction will legitimately open out onto a new lack. It is justified only as a 'leaky cask'.

When Callicles therefore opposes insatiable hunger to the 'wisdom' to which Socrates wants to lead us, teaching us to consider ourselves as 'full' and to be content, knowing how to limit our desires and consider them satisfied, we should not mistake his intention—

it is not to praise a life lived without restraint, in debauchery and excess, something which Socrates tried to make him feel ashamed of by descending ever further into the realm of needs to relieve (of when 'one has the itch', 'scratches', and so on). Under cover of this affirmed intemperance, *akolastia*, something else is actually in play. The question is: Where should the plenitude of life be situated? Is it in the given *result* when desire will thereby be gratified—the entry into port, harbour or success? But then, no longer being projected ahead of oneself through a lack, one no longer needs to live—this harbour is, however, death. Or, rather, the plenitude of life will be situated in the *in progress* of life, implying a renewal which is itself possible only if all filling up is at the same time an emptying out, all gratification an escape? Will it be situated in the peace of coveted satisfaction or, rather, in the tension of an activity which refuses to accept that desire should be limited in order not to have to stop? Socrates denounces the illusory character of a life constrained to repeat itself due to what it lacks; but, under the appearance of exempting us from it, he causes us to miss nothing less, as Callicles boldly retorts, than life's characteristic capacity to be alive.

In fact, we can easily see that Plato does not know how to give consistency to this 'between' (desire and satiety) which constitutes life's being *in progress*. Socrates has so effectively tied one to the other, the filling and the emptying, inexorably chaining them together, that it is only in the gratification of a lack that he can perceive exhilaration (at least, exhilaration of the body). He is so much under the influence of the conception, and, above all, of the formulation, according to which all desire is a 'desire for' (the object that is lacking) that he does not appear even to conceive of a desire, or, consequently, pleasure that might no longer be under the pressure of lack but which begins with its release. 'The pleasure of drinking,' he insists as though this was evidence, 'ceases for each of us with thirst' (*Gorgias*, 49). This time, Callicles weakly acquiesces. Having until this moment been so combative, he now allows himself to get caught in the trap of the idea that satisfaction is only obtained from privation, and of having no future except its return— possessing, in short, no other extension except a negative one of a fresh lack to be gratified or another form of suffering to be relieved. It is as if, once it has been staunched, nothing more remains than to wait for thirst to appear once more, as if the real pleasure of drinking does not start when we are plagued with thirst but that, as the want is satisfied, as the pressure of the need is absorbed, one starts to drink 'for the sake of drinking', even without being thirsty and simply in order to *taste* (a quality). It is no longer to gratify a lack but to savour, the savouring not being able properly to begin except by taking off from lack, therefore *from the vicinities* of satiety. Because, as we know, satiety is not of itself a whole—it is not a halt, a stoppage, but a development which draws out at length, as a dotted line.

Not only does Socrates not conceive of tangency between the two, still less one that would be an asymptote of the slender right of desire for the curvilinear withdrawal of satisfaction, so prolonging their *between* indefinitely; not only does he not envisage even some interstice or shading in this infernal cycle of wastage-repletion constantly renewing itself, but he also conceives this intermediary time between privation and satisfaction less as a transition leading from one to the other than as a rupture—this *between* once more having escaped. The non-coincidence between the present state of lack (which still continues) and the future state of satisfaction (to which one aspires) is explained solely through the dualism of body and soul and not as a process—while the body is closed in the present of the sensation, the soul anticipates the satisfaction to come because it remembers the (same) past satisfaction (*Philebus*: 31–6; see Dixsaut 1999: 245).

This passage from lack to satisfaction is thus conceived less itself as a passage than as the overflowing of a (psychological) capacity in relation to the (physiological) other operating by memory and projection. Admittedly, without memory there would be no desire, Plato affirms, and what is living would find itself condemned to being enclosed in the present time (of the body). But the memory with which the soul is endowed liberates what is living from the present only so as to immediately imprison it in the linkage of opposites, since, when the body experiences lack, the soul can only anticipate the contrary state— of satisfaction—which it remembers. Thanks to the memory of the soul, what is living is certainly no longer cloistered in the corporeal cycle and can emancipate itself from the present moment. But as the desired state is always a memorized state, desire (which is always that of the soul) turns in a circle, Plato concludes, finding a future only in the past.

In other words, Plato did not conceive of there being any interest in this *between* (in which life happens). Thinking of this life of the living only as a succession of depletion and repletion (hunger, thirst), thereby enclosing the activity of the living in the sequence of dissolution and reconstitution of physiological harmony (*Philebus*: 31d), Plato can legitimately only make us aspire to an *other life*, one that is 'more divine', having faith in the soul alone and its 'theoretical' knowledge; become impassive and liberated from this cycle, these pure pleasures of the mind alone bring us closer to what is 'on the other side' (from 'true life'). Life is devoted from the outset to what its 'end' might be (*telos*), in the full sense of the Greek word— at once a conclusion, aim and perfection, and abandoning all the preceding *between* of life to indifference. A return is made, once again, to those principal categories upon which Socrates settled, as if on a definitive experience (*Philebus*: 54c–e)—having in view only what arises from the essence (*ousia*) and has an ontological status, and forsaking from the outset whatever is of the order of becoming, the *genesis*, in such a way that, between desire and satisfaction, such a life henceforth cannot be envisaged except as dependent upon this materialization, drawn in by this going beyond—and therefore intrinsically unable to possess value.

It has similarly been endlessly repeated since the time of Nietzsche: Plato in this way turned aside from the development of life and the perceptible for the *beyond* of another life, and the cost that life has paid has been great. I wonder: Can we really be satisfied with this endlessly repeated denunciation? And how did Plato effectively come to the point of obliterating thought of process, of all process, above all that of life, to this rejection of *genesis*, of finding no solution except through a perilous leap into the 'theoretical' and the postulation of the 'ideal'? Why would Plato have desired to flee this life of the living for the life that comes after death or in the 'place of ideas'? I suppose that it is less due to rejecting the present of life and giving into the resentment ostensibly distilled by Socrates than a philosophical or, more accurately, logical, incapacity to think through what is *between* desire and satiety—consequently, doubtless more for want of a tool than by conversion. At least, being more suspicious, we can start to read Plato between the lines and not directly, through what we perceive him to have been lacking and not simply from what he expounds. It is because he did not (or could not) know how to give a consistent status to the 'between' (*metaxu*) that he had to construct in the 'Beyond', the meta of metaphysics. It was there that he would find himself at ease and able to construct. Is everything else, including the famous 'ascetic' values so often denounced, worthwhile only by virtue of its consequence?

2

Have we in fact ever emerged from a kind of logical *trapdoor* by which European thought has found itself captured due to an incapacity to think through the *between* (of life)? Just like that, this contradiction closes up over what we then call *existence* and condemns it (with no further escape possible): Do we perceive the slightest start of an alternative? Would not anything with a claim to elude it just be a fear of thinking about it? As hunger would teach us, we justify our incessant action only through the projected acquisition of what we lack but which, once obtained, immediately disappoints us and throws us back upon a fresh hunger. In Pascalian terms: we believe that, having come to the end of the difficulties we have encountered before attaining this aim, we will finally attain the rest we covet, that of satiety, without ourselves taking into account (or, rather, desperately wanting to hide from ourselves) the fact that, once this object of satisfaction has been attained, we would no longer be able to tolerate the sense of relaxation into which such satisfaction has plunged us, insofar as this rest is 'boring'; and that we have an incontinent need for a fresh object of lack and 'excitement'. In this game, we hold passionately to the gain which thrills us—if there is nothing to gain or if this gain would from the outset be accorded to us, the play holds no interest for us; but the gain ceases to interest us once it has been attained—we become 'drunk' on it.

Pascal and classical psychology as a whole were masters in the art of demonstrating that all attainment is a snare, that all *satisfaction* is *disappointing*. If you do not acknowledge it, it is because you do not 'see', do not want to 'know', not wanting to think about it and preferring to deceive yourself. Or perhaps it is better to deceive yourself in this way—otherwise, life would be unbearable. We have left there the elementary and physiological cycle of vital loss-restoration, which Plato denounced; 'hunger' has now become an internal void (through the Christian deployment of the form of the Subject). But the coercive logic of the sequence remains—the trapdoor really has been shut. Or (the *or* of the only way out), once this slipknot has been placed around our necks, we are led back to the great consolatory (because redemptive) Narrative which alone is able to unravel the contradiction through its montage and its promise of the true life elsewhere—the fact that we aspire towards the serenity of acquisition is the trace of the original nature we have lost, concludes Pascal; and the fact that we are only able to live in 'agitation' is the mark of the Fall and of our corrupted nature.

It is true: today, we would gladly claim to have untied ourselves from this great religious *muthos*—but is one so easily liberated from the argument underlying it? If not, then what is this proclaimed freeing worth? With satisfaction equivalent to disappointment, has their vice been loosened? In other words, will we ever stop being Pascalians, a Pascalian that each of us in Europe discovers within our own hearts as soon as we scratch the surface? Nietzsche himself was marked by it, admiring the psychological perspicacity which is unafraid of casting a glance into the abyss and mocking procrastination.[5] We become this Pascalian as soon as we read the *Pensées*, in our youth, caught as we are by both the geometrical rigour of the reasoning and the intimacy of the appeal we hear in it. Otherwise, we would be at risk of surreptitiously lapsing into a feeble 'Voltairian' discourse which will do no more than take the edge off its trenchancy, chip a corner from its outline while balancing its lucidity with resignation or, rather, temper its radicality with a smile while conducts the gaze elsewhere, the leaves growing or the joy of children; or, simply, praise 'activity'—but without being able to reverse it—avoiding neither the withdrawal (into compromise) nor the denial (before the vanity of existence). With Pascal, in fact, as he said himself, the 'bullet' is 'well placed'. Could we detach ourselves from his analysis of 'amusement', of the hunt and the game, and of the king abandoned to himself, at the heart of his magnificence, although we gladly recognize it: 'We never look for things, but go in search of them.' And our nature, if we have one, lies in 'movement' (Pascal).

I would nevertheless like to begin with a rejoinder, by retracing our steps and rereading this analysis (Voltaire's response is so feeble because it is without a concept to oppose)—that it is the 'hunt', and not the 'capture', to which we are attached, is only the proof that it is the hunt, in fact, which counts, opening the *between* to our activity (between the quest and its satisfaction); and the capture is from that point only a pretext that serves as little more than an edge or support for this 'between' of the occupation through which life is deployed. Why should it be necessary to privilege the goal, the conclusion (the 'relaxation'), to the detriment of the whole of the preceding time which is then no longer considered except as having to lead to it, annulling itself in this materialization? Unless it is, once again, due to the idealist valorization of metaphysics (thinking in terms of 'being' as opposed to becoming, stability and identity) upon which Christian thought, having become dogmatic, is also propped up. According to Pascal, the 'tumult' of existence (its 'disturbance', 'bustle', 'worry') will then necessarily and negatively be opposed to them.... So much so that, in being unable to know how to accord a positive status to the *between*, we cannot emerge from the insidious connotation of 'agitation'.

This Pascalian development, carried to perfection in the way we know, is therefore no less to be taken up again in order to purchase what tendentiously is mingled in it and circumvents us in an adroit way and under cover of analysis. In the same way, do we not see in this one of the first (and most beautiful) 'existential' analyses? I would then like to know: Is the person who acts to obtain what will unquestionably fail to satisfy him, *but after the event*, for all that a dupe? Perhaps he is a dupe without being duped— the hunter (the player) is, fundamentally, complicit (aware) in his delusion because he knows that this 'fundamentally' cannot be dug out, that it is perhaps this 'fundamental' that is the fiction. He is, likewise, neither pretending (when he wants the capture by running after the hare) nor denying that the capture would finally be unsatisfying—for the moment that follows does not at all efface what has gone before (the *between* of the activity). It *is not its truth*. Whoever gets hooked on the game deploys his capacities but (then) need not be embarrassed when this goal is found 'after all' to be secondary.

For as soon as the plenitude is seen within the substantial *between* of the activity, and no longer in what one has aimed at obtaining, an action (occasion) is no longer perceived as illusory nor its stake as derisory. Or, if we are deceived, it is rather in the way in which we have learnt to think about the aim, that is, as an *end* upon which everything depends, and not only as a prospective, even fictive, support of activity, that keeps us in suspense and in process, so hegemonic has been its consecration by philosophy. Our eyes are opened, in fact, but onto what? Claiming to disabuse us, Pascal deceives us more subtly still by leading us retrospectively to forget (according to the smooth, equal, level, abraded time of the metaphysic) that this *moment* (of the hunt, of pleasure, of intensity) has well and truly existed. Ineffaceable and comparable to nothing else, it exists as nothing more could exist, filled as it is by its occurrence. In relation to this, the conclusion that is so coveted is simply the condition of possibility that has been posed in advance, and not the justification.

Christian (Jansenist) 'pessimism', it has been said of these pages, in order to dismiss it—these folk at Port-Royal are obsessed by the idea of humanity's 'misfortune' and have not known how to take their minds off it, to look up or to the side. But, in fact, the characteristic of Pascalian thought, and what give it its force, is that it no longer allows the 'to the side' to subsist. 'To the side' is wrong—it means flight, avoidance, returning itself into the inexorable logic of 'amusement'. Hence, that for want of being able to produce a counter-discourse, European humanism routinely and surreptitiously returns to it as soon as it is constructed, is somewhat serious. It remains haunted by what it has remained unable to capture, in relation to which it therefore does not know how to take the opposite direction—even if it only admits it in an aside: that the problem posed by life, and its pain, is not so much that happiness would be 'unattainable' (that would be placing the bar too high) but that it would be *unbearable*; not that happiness would be impossible but that it would be boring. For hardly has this coveted happiness been attained than one becomes tired of it. Goethe: 'Nothing is harder to bear / than a succession of fair days.' And Freud, in citing Goethe: 'When any situation that is desired by the pleasure principle is prolonged, it only produces a feeling of mild contentment. We are so made that we can derive intense enjoyment only from a contrast and very little from a state of things' (Freud 1961).

It is therefore not the fact that the world refuses to satisfy our desire, something in step with the 'reality principle', which would be alarming, even if this was what we would like to believe (the negative would be only external); but that, by our own constitution, satisfaction comes apart of its own accord in the duration it has nevertheless coveted: 'Complexion,' says Pascal; 'Constitution,' says Freud—the old myth of human nature is still ineradicably there, to raise in conflict, in the absolute, that which would be, on the one hand, our aspiration (in rest: that which is a 'state') and, on the other, our undeniable need for variation and contrast. But who says that it would necessarily be this state ('of rest') that we have to enjoy, that is to say, perpetually, according to philosophy, of the restoration of an order which at once would be posed as a goal (of the 'programme of pleasure') and be sustainable? Why not the changing (unstable) being deployed in the *between* (of activity) and in relation to which the rest in sight is only an ideal support serving, again by contrast, motivation and whose character would be revealed after the (*temporary*) fictive event as fundamentally of little concern? But why, when he cites the formula of Goethe in a note (to add a note is already, as we know, to admit a gap into the continuity of the discussion), did Freud, ordinarily so radical, also need to erode its sharpness? It is as if he had no other way of taking it apart: 'But this may be an exaggeration' (ibid.). Why therefore take a step back in such a flat, and unconvincing, way no sooner has the thesis been put forward? Does not this retraction *ultimately* call for denial? Does Freud tiptoe back from this because of what he might be so dangerously close to—vertigo? He too is led, without recourse or help, to what seems to be the only remaining and prudent stratagem when confronted with the abrupt thesis of humanity's 'misfortune'—to dodge it.

3

This ideological bolt is so well shut on European consciousness that it has not only taken on a logical form (from the ideological to the logical, this is really the consecution, rather than the inverse) but it also blocks our imaginary realm. Without even investing further belief in it, we wonder: How should the lives of contented souls reaching their end, near to God and in their coveted *telos*, be conceived? The earlier contradiction, transferred to an ideal plane, still haunts us. In effect, let us turn all human limits and the 'poverty' of our condition into an abstraction. Could we go beyond this incompatibility of the *desire* which, once gratified, becomes *disgust*? Even near to God, if we transport our life into a blessed future, either the privation still engenders suffering; or satisfaction, inversely, can only generate boredom—hence the well-known difficulty of representing 'paradise'. The theologians have tried to do so in turn but have been able to do nothing about it. How else could the lives of souls be represented in the redemptive beyond except by confronting this alternative? Either, raised up to God, they still experience the desire for God, but this leaves them still in a state of want and therefore unsatisfied and consequently unhappy; or they are gratified by the presence of God. But, in this case, how could this satiety, which consequently is non-desire, fail to be transformed into lassitude? In the words of Augustine: 'If I say that you will not satisfied, it means that you would have been hungry; if I say that you will be satisfied, I fear your loathing' (*Confessions*: 3.21).

Likewise, however one understands this Origenian thesis advanced by the first spiritual individuals who, gripped with satiety in contemplation of God, would consequently 'turn away' from him (according to this provocative expression: 'to have a satiety of divine vision', *koron labein tes theôrias*) (Harl 1993), this is no less the result—that the theologian, as soon as he is satisfied with the idea of rest and stability as characterizing the absolute perfection of a happy life, cannot avoid having to think about this untenable state. Could there, in fact, be a satiety of good, *satietas beni*, as there is a satiety of evil? Or is it then necessary to assume, along with Gregory of Nyssa, that the only possible way of avoiding this difficulty would be if, even when close to God, the souls of the blessed remain hungry for him in order to preserve their appetite for him. But how then could they be 'blessed'? 'Therefore, what he desires to accomplish for Moses through doing so, his desire remains unsatisfied' (1978: §63.1). More precisely and without absorbing the shock of the Greek words—what he desires 'is filled' (*plerôutai*) due to the very fact that his desire is 'not full' (*aplerôtos*). We understand that God satisfies the one who seeks Him according to his capacity, and augments the capacity in proportion of the one who finds Him, but what happens when we reach this ultimate state 'in which we will be so fulfilled that our capacity could not be increased' (*Confessions:* 63.1)? Will our perfection therefore no longer be susceptible to any progress? Once this ultimate state is attained, how can we imagine that this appetite will not be vexed, that this appeasement will not reverse into 'disgust'? Or will it not become necessary, once again, to take refuge in the oxymoron in order to sidestep it with a non sequitur? 'Insatiable satiety,' says Augustine, *insatiabilis satietas*, parallel to the *invisibilis visio* of God. But the oxymoron, let us repeat, does not think.

4

We would like to open another possibility, but how—how to go about breaking open the vice which holds us in its grip to the extent of our capacity to conceive of the ideal life (paradise)? What could a counter-discourse, should we wish to find one, take support from, since the option here is anchored so much in the point that serves as backdrop to our imagination? Or what other logical possibility would remain to loosen the blockage that has been instigated at least since Platonism than deliberately to hold back from this *always pouring* as from this *definitive gratification*, or from insatiable hunger and disappointing satiety, posed in the extreme terms of vitality? Or to avoid letting ourselves be overcome (and fascinated) by the passage to the limit, dropping the 'between' of the transition, since it certainly eludes the mind through its indetermination? But does truth lie in the determination? And is life necessarily reached by means of 'truth'?

A Chinese formula warns us against this mirage of the rest-state as against the extremity which marks. It shelters us from this overly brutal light which the antipodes would pour out. It discretely shifts us away from this rut by no longer sweeping this *between* of occupation under the oblique carpet:

To pour without filling,
To draw without ever exhausting.

For the *tao*, the 'way', the *Zhuangzi* already alerts us, as a prerequisite, 'without demarcation' (*wei shi you feng*; Guo 1983: Chapter 2): the *tao* which 'gleams', which comes loose, 'is not the *tao*'; and, in the same way, 'the word which distinguishes does not attain'. In other words, what is most characterizable is also what is most arbitrary. On the contrary, the *tao*, the 'way', expresses the *between* which does not immobilize itself from any side as it ceaselessly allows a way through. This is not the way leading to something (to a *telos* or coveted end), but the way of 'viability' by which the *continuum* of life is renewed. But this is also why the *tao* can only be described as 'hazy', 'vague' or indeterminate—it is not of 'Being'.

Let's set the scene: the same formula is found between two conceptual characters of the Taoist Master (*Zhuangzi*, Chapter 12 in ibid.). 'Obscure authenticity' (insofar as it is possible to translate its name) yields to the East, in the 'ample valley'—it will encounter a 'fecund wind' on the seashore. I go into the 'ample valley', it says. But what is this? 'It is, as reality, that which we pour without ever filling, from which we draw without exhausting. I will advance from there.' Where one does not pour to the point of filling nor draw to the point of drying up, these extreme, dramatic states of (painful) lack or (boring) gratification will no longer be encountered. *Tao*, the 'way', already expressed the renewal of a passage—when one makes 'use' of it—which through its 'evident median' (*chong dao*) never results in gratification: 'Taking off the sharp edges' as 'equalizing the light' (*Laozi*: §4). Then, in the same way, *to advance* (*you*) is a word which means precisely, through the effacement of extremities and without any establishment of an end or a destination, the variation 'by one's will' in the interval—which keeps in motion, animated, but without there being any further urgent 'towards something' to which I aspire, without fixation or contraction from any side. The sage 'advances' into the *tao*, it is said, 'as do fishes in water'.

Let us therefore pursue this three-sided exchange. In the tense and inconclusive dialogue between Socrates and Callicles (one of the most violent, we might say, of the Greek stage), let us introduce this other voice. Brim-full casks are worth more, says Socrates—this 'fullness' frees us. But, says Callicles, casks that are full of holes, into which we pour again and again, this 'pouring' alone holds us in life. Now the Taoist thinker, purely by balancing his formula, unjams this choice, taking apart or, rather, *relaxing* the antagonism. In order to do this, all that is necessary is to listen to the balancing alternation the sentence produces, as one word responds to the other and both hold back from the extremity—pouring without filling; drawing but without exhausting. This formula is sufficient to make its respiration clear, in its continual exchange, as it renews itself from one to the other but does not go to the end of either one, for the one already calls upon the other, and, refraining from untenable states, also refrains from disjunction (*either* totally empty or totally full), the *respiration* is what effectively holds in the interval. It is always of the moment (it cannot be before or after). By virtue of this, it is exemplary of the contemporary capacity of living. Was it not necessary, in fact, to change paradigms in order to emerge from this jamming? It is, consequently, the respiration which most fundamentally makes the argument against the blockage in both positions—something it has not occurred to European philosophy to think about, as we discover by divergence.

Let's not give in to the fascination for a toughening up, says the Taoist, as though within this we could finally reveal the truth (or, if it remains interdependent with the extreme, let's challenge ourselves with the truth). In other words, let us not naively think that *by touching the extremity* we might know it. Neither that of the void calling for a relentless pouring out, nor that of a fullness as restful as if one had already passed away. Let us avoid the critical state, on both sides, and let us be careful about the 'reservation' or the withdrawal—the ground without ground of the *tao*—of the two sides. In keeping to this side of the boundary, without 'leaving' or 'attaching', in other words, without sinking into it, any more than depriving yourself of it, but in illuminating this *between* of activity, you would avoid hypostasizing one or other arising as an alternative (responds Zhuangzi)—as much the hunger avid with desire (Callicles) as the satiety of repose (Socrates); you would escape the suffering of destitution as well as the disgust of gratification.

Likewise, under this encouragement that is oblique but as good as an invitation, without for all that having the weight of a thesis, it will not at all be necessary to fear reversing the perspective—to take up once more the prejudices perhaps too hastily sealed up by philosophy. Let us no longer consider the *between* as what, left without concept and limited to separating extremes, is of value only as an interval that is easy for thought to step over and recognize from the outset as less intense. Let us no longer see it as this relative, condemned at least by its vagueness to a lesser existence while the two extremities, alone determined (as *eidé*, the Greek says), touch the absolute. Instead, let us leave these two borders as dotted lines, but whose toughness we know can so easily be accentuated, as the condition of possibility of this *between* in which everything finally happens, above all this continual transition that is the respiration of life. Life and death, striking us by their event, 'are', in truth, only to bring to light the *occasion* of life. Would it be going too far to consider the reversal valorizing this discreet *between*, to the detriment of the dramatic noise of the Extremities, is signalled to us in a muted way as one of the great contemporary ideological mutations? We would have understood, all in all, that it is not the passage to the extreme which illuminates; that the truth is not to be found concealed within the extremity; and that no doubt it is really this that would, above all, distance us from metaphysics.

We have come to the time of the *holding-between*;[6] in other words, where we hold to the between, where we hold it from the between, where we know that it is in the *between* of demarcations that this capacity is discerned; that the effective develops. More generally, it is in the aptitude to *open what is between* that life is deployed; and above all between future and past which otherwise would reduce this present, as we know, to a pure mathematical point, without extension, therefore without existence; the 'present', properly speaking, does not 'exist'; it is promoted and gathered by separating the future and the past from each other, rejecting them from both sides, like a dotted line. 'Holding-between' is the concept to be developed which needs, from being a technique, to become an ethic. We say that a transversal beam 'holds-between' the framework as it holds it together through the median tension it exerts. From this, *holding-between* means to keep active by arranging this intervening period: a holding maintenance of the world (in which one is finally placed); holding conversations with others (which is not made up of words alone); a holding maintenance of life (although how could this be limited to the physical—respiration itself is not limited to it?). It is not that, having passed through the age of projects and adventures, a step would be taken back from the danger of the extreme or that, having been shoved against the windows, we return prudently near the centre, humming to ourselves. No, but we understand that to give in to the vertigo of the End is all too easy.

5

In a certain way, however, Plato had given consistency to the *formless* 'between' of the transition—as the 'mixing' of opposites. Let us return to these primary cases of hunger and thirst: when I drink, being thirsty, I experience at once pain (of thirst) and pleasure (of the pouring—*Gorgias*: 496e). Indeed, the analysis of the 'intermediary' (*en mesôi*) can be refined, by differentiating in the simultaneity of time—I still suffer from being thirsty but I remember at the same time the pleasure (in the past) which will put a stop to my suffering (in the future), in proportion as I drink (*Philebus*: 35e). I experience at the same time a painful feeling and rejoice in advance and the bitterness is mingled with sweetness. So Plato does not draw back from this contradiction which is raised at the level of experience—he finds a place for it. He even extends this mix to the feelings of the soul alone: when we experience a 'derisive wish' or laugh at the absurdities of our friends, does not reasoning simply show us that, mingling pleasure in rejection, we allow opposites to coexist (*Philebus*: 49–50)? In tragic spectacle, 'do we not enjoy our tears' (48a)? What 'unheard of composite', of pain and joy at once, did not the disciples experience when faced with the death of Socrates, as serene as it was (*Phaedo*: 59a)?

But what is a 'mix' (*meixis, krasis*)? If Plato, a fine psychologist, is good at discerning how, in each case, the one is closely mingled with the other (pleasure with pain or bitterness with sweetness), he does not for all that question that they remain opposed—there is mingling but not confusion to such a point that it is no longer possible to distinguish one from the other in its principle. Joy and pain are associated contradictorily in the same subject, but one is not allowed to be harmed or diluted by the other; one remains impervious to the other due to its determinations; hence they can be analysed by dissociating them at the very heart of their mingling and 'interlacing'. In other words, this *mingling* does not entail *ambiguity*— the fact that the opposed coexist does not mean, by the same token, that the frontier between them will be erased, revealing in this *between* a secret community such as to render the demarcation indecisive. An 'ambiguous' victory is a victory which can veer towards one sense as well as towards another, keeping them indivisible and not cut apart. Descending from the ideal life to the life of man, Plato is the thinker of the mingling and not of the ambiguity.

From the *mix*, Plato has no difficulty in getting to *exclusion*. If, in the obscurity of affects, joy and pain can be mingled, the same thing is not so for health and sickness and still less for happiness and unhappiness, or good and evil (*Gorgias*: 495–6). Or, again, at the beginning of the *Phaedo*, Socrates, when he has his chains taken off, takes pleasure in scratching himself and is amazed at the extent to which pain and pleasure are linked, as though they are joined 'by a single head', although the dialogue goes on to demonstrate, as it elaborates nothing less than the theory of 'ideas', how opposed essences, just like their first qualities, are incompatible. Therefore the more I detach myself from the perceptible and the affective, the more I approach at once Being and clarity, the more I elevate myself to the ideal and the more I also consequently measure the incompatibility of opposites. This causes me to wonder if this is not the real reason Plato thought in terms of 'Being' and *gave up on life*. Since the level of Being is the one where the distinction of essences can be conveniently operated, each, through its determination, withdraws into itself and encloses itself in its property (the in-self-as-self of its uniqueness), even though thinking about life forces us on the contrary to descend to this *fundamental(s) of ambiguity* (of obscurity) where each is no longer certain of being able to be differentiated from its opposite and may even proceed from it. This is what Plato resolutely overturns. He wants to rise up to the light.

When thereby, enamoured of logical relationships, we ask ourselves about what has caused the greatest cleavage in the history of thought, even if it is left relatively indistinct (and does not directly emerge, specifically, on the surface of the philosophical subject), around which the debate therefore turns too narrowly in order to reflect it, I believe one will be able to return from it to this point—it is here that the knife passes: Plato takes pleasure in describing the mixing but, for all that, does not go back to the question of the identity of what is mixed; he really wants the opposites to be linked in a contradictory way to each other, entangled but not so much that they take each other apart. There really is, all in all, some 'between' at work, as a simultaneous coexistence of contraries, at once joy and pain, pleasure and suffering. However, this *between* does not cause them to communicate—it keeps them watertight. Whatever entangling they might end up with in life, they remain separable by right; and the level of Being, at which Plato has perched thought, is the place where this legitimate distinction is illuminated and read (as the 'separation of essences', *diairesis tôn eidôn*).

If we want to place philosophy in front of its implicit prejudices, I believe we will be unable to avoid asking ourselves whether mixing (maintaining the principle of difference) would not be the ambiguity (no longer deciding between opposites) and that, by thinking about Being (the in-self, the identical, the determined), we are discharging ourselves from thinking, not so much about shifts or variegation as, more precisely, from the *ambiguity* characteristic of life (and even that one might choose to think about 'Being' in order to be discharged from having to think about life, postponing this 'essence' of life into another life, one that is refined and divested of any ambiguity). Is this not what has been the great burden of weight-choice-destiny for Western philosophy erected as metaphysics? In this way what the edification of metaphysics, drawing into the light the incompatibilities of essences and constructing from them the logical play of relations, has put to one side or rejected into the shadows, it would fall to literature in Europe to gather, recuperating what had thereby been lost of the equivocal nature and ambivalence of Being deployed in the ancient *muthos*.

Literature draws its justification from this, but at the cost, in Europe, of some cultural schizophrenia that we barely analyse, just as this rivalry, between both 'literature' and 'philosophy', has deployed their respective resources to the point of exasperation. On what *tacit reason* does literature rest, a serious reason, if it is only in the ambiguity chased out of the *logos*, more still than in the singular or the imaginary, or the narrative or the emotive, which are after all only modalities serving to retain and safeguard this characteristic ambiguity of life, that it finds its vocation and compensatory function? Consequently, there is a sharing of roles, due to object and pertinence, but which, with philosophy having weakened its position, is precisely effaced today: on the one hand, philosophy, as it builds antinomies against the background (*fond*) of Being, has founded the possibility of knowledge, as well as moral choice and therefore of Freedom (its great theoretical tryptique); on the other hand, literature, by preserving the ambiguity and arranging the half-light in which opposites communicate and understand each other through hints from within, but without consequently completely confessing it, or at least without theorizing it (what tool could it use?), is 'concerned' with life.

The novelist does not so much distinguish the mingling of feelings, according to his supposed talent as a psychologist, and playing with the anatomist's knife, as he allows a hint of how the 'same' feeling (or sensation or quality) can remain in the *between*, indecisive in respect of its rival orientations and ready again to tip over from one into the other—not so much by indetermination as by reticence about allowing them to be differentiated and isolated into so-called contraries. This occurs to such a point that, even specifically affirmed, such a feeling does not break the affinity with its other; it never even reveals itself as being as close to an other as to its opposite. A character 'lives' not so much because his feelings are complex (once again the mingling) as because they allow a glimpse (but in way that is dangerous for clear thinking attached to antinomies) of the foundation(s) (*fond*[*s*]) upon which one turns into its opposite and keeps them in communication with each other, one of them therefore still wandering in its other and never completely allowing itself to be ousted. For example, not settling between the ambition, *alias* the personal revenge of a solitary revolt, *and* the infinite tenderness ready to sacrifice itself (Julien Sorel in comparison with Mme de Rênal).

6

This was precisely what Nietzsche seized upon in order to undermine the enterprise of metaphysics and denounce the way it has renounced life: instead of opposing one to the other in an antinomical way, dramatically setting up the scene of their exclusion, owing to their necessary disjunction, and, consequently, that of moral choice, as though they could demand inverse origins ('celestial' and 'terrestrial'; 'sensible' and 'suprasensible'), do not our contraries rather 'proceed' from both (*entstehen*) and do they not remain, in fact, secretly complicit (on the page, one of the strongest in all of Nietzsche, that opens *Beyond Good and Evil* [1968a])? What link kept hidden, or subterranean tunnel, connects, for example, 'disinterested action' and 'egoism' (or truth and error, or the contemplation of the wise man and covetousness, and so on) from within, behind the scenes—keeping each of these couples in the ambiguity of indivisibility, in spite of the expulsion so solemnly pronounced?

To think about life would therefore imply this radical change of perspective passing from metaphysical edification to genealogical suspicion. No longer founding opposites in Being, they will henceforth be considered only as fixed extreme states, as phenomena which, when considered more closely, are revealed as gradual and reversible. These are the qualities whose points of passage we neglect, of which we fail to appreciate the delicate *between* of transition and due to which we block them off as antagonistic essences, as though they arose from opposed worlds, as though this nuanced *between* was simply the iridescence of an appearance (the one denounced by ontology); and that truth was to be sought simply in what is *clear-cut*. Again, it seems to me that Nietzsche does not sufficiently distinguish one from the other: on the one hand, the 'entangling' (maintaining difference, *verknüpft*, once again the mingling); and, on the other, the 'uniting' and even the 'identity of essence' (*vervwandt*, *wesensgleich*), reducing the separation to the point of extending the confusion and obscuring all identity. Again, Nietzsche remains in the 'dangerous perhaps' (*gefürhrliches vielleicht*), sufficient to break open the bolt of antinomies, through his daring hypothesis, while precipitating, through his challenge, the reversal of values but without wanting (or being able) to explore further this common fund of ambiguity (the source or founding, *fons* or *fundus*) from where life arises before beginning to split itself up, or that we unduly oppose to itself.

It will certainly be retorted to this massive charge cast against metaphysics that, from the beginning metaphysics was allowed to be infiltrated by the eventuality of its subversion, that all great philosophy reveals the anxiety of what threatens it (this is precisely how we recognize a 'great' philosophy), and that Plato himself, the first great constructor of ontology, at least once approached this point that is the most perilous of all because it undermines the very possibility of ontology (famously as a 'parricide'), where Being is also revealed to 'be' its opposite; that, wanting to grasp the ungraspable nature of what most resists it, that of the 'Sophist', of what is only an image or a semblance camouflaging itself in the shadowy interval between being and non-being, he allows himself to be fascinated by this explosive enunciation which henceforth becomes necessary, that 'non-being', under a certain relation, 'exists' and that 'being', in some way, does not 'exist' (*The Sophist*: 241d). An earthquake in Greek thought: On the track of this game that eludes capture and becomes impossible to drive out, would we finally emerge from the thinking of the mixing, crossing and interlacing of contraries (*meixis, epallaxis, sumploké*) while respecting their properties? A dizzy moment if ever there was one: Would the distinction of principle between one and the other begin to vacillate to the point that the one no longer simply intermingles with its other, even in an inextricable way, but *takes itself apart* in it? This would then be to the point that, their separation having become evasive, from underneath the definitive quality of Being, the one going back into its foundations to the point of passing into its opposite, might the ambiguity (of life)—disclosed—finally be able to appear?

Plato, it is true, is here skirting the very edge of the precipice on which, with the one communicating surreptitiously with its opposite, *identity* could be abolished or at least tied up; where one would begin to glimpse Being begin, like an abyss, these ground-less foundations of ambiguity; where the *between* would no longer be purely relational but allow an indiscernability of the demarcation to come to light against which all determination by the word would then break. But if, in order not to fall into what was the greatest danger, we know that Plato produced nothing less than the magisterial tool of the dialectic (the only thing equal to the risk incurred), it was really to allow a 'participation' between essences, but still preserving their reciprocal 'externality' (*ektos toutôn*, *The Sophist*: 250d). His masterstroke, or the only way out, was to think of negation as expressing the 'other', but not the contrary, in such a way that 'non-being' would cease to be the contrary of 'being' but be the very other of 'being', and therefore no longer be in contradiction to it, which is how the 'other' thereby becomes erected as a proper 'genus', equal in every respect, the partner of others and mediator of their relation and therefore no longer threatening them from within.

This time the principle is re-established by which the opposites, if they participate in an 'other', cannot in any case communicate with each other—the exclusion of contraries is maintained and the antinomy is safe. Because of this the function of the mingling is also re-established, and even 'finally' grounded (*fondée*), since it would from that point pass under the jurisdiction of the dialectician on the alert to ensure that this mingling between genera will be properly respected. The correct predication is thereby found to be legitimated and, consequently, a normative use of the discourse is established, equally avoiding being able to say nothing about nothing or everything about everything, or that one would be caught in the tautology or delivered to the delirium of a word in freewheel—philosophy purges itself once and for all of the ambiguity of the *between*, which would place the methodological distinction of essences in peril, or, at least, repress it into the realm of the unthought.

The same would happen with Hegel, the other grand master of dialectic, at the other end of the history of *logos*—a dialectic no longer content to think about how the one, in a certain way, 'is' also the other (to ground/found [*fonder*] the possibility of predication), how the one necessarily 'passes' into its other (founding for modernity the possibility of History as a becoming of the Subject). But Hegel also comes as close as possible to the fire that consumes identities. When, emerging from a logic of antinomic and disjunctive 'understanding', he thought about contraries no longer as 'one outside the other' but such that each 'becomes other to itself', he once again comes near to the precipice on which oppositions, one opening on its other, become undone, where an inexpugnable fund of ambiguity appears—and it is really the 'fluidity' of 'life' that Hegel is actually thinking about.

But, here again, the dialectic is that tool which allows the zone of turbulence to be overcome without allowing ourselves to be carried away and with our gaze already fixed on its surpassing. In this way, the other is prevented from irradiating at the heart of the same, crammed as it already is by finality. Admittedly, the same sees itself disappropriated from itself, rendered 'unequal' to itself, and now the negative really works from within. However, this other, serving the same, does not contaminate it—passed through by it, (the *dia* of the dialectic), it neither opens it out nor overcomes it. With this 'other' now under tutelage, the dialectic once again saves us from the gulf into which, demarcation proving to be impossible, the one would no longer be split from its other but would be understand within it. Too 'dangerous perhaps'; in fact, only Nietzsche, blocking the path to dialectization, has supported it. But can we be satisfied with such a dangerous 'perhaps'?

7

Let us in fact raise the Nietzschean question afresh, not this time as this final arrow, the most daring, risky and poisoned one, discharged in haste against moralism in the process of withdrawal (the Parthian shot), or as if lifting a last veil cast over the imposture of the ideal. Let us stay within range, but turn the target around. It then reveals, on this side of the codifications and demarcations of morality, that *fund of ambiguity* which alone enables us to understand that life can unfold in one direction equally well as in its contrary, and maintains them in a strange affinity. How, asks Nietzsche without analysing it, can disinterested action (*die selbstlose Handlung*) proceed from egoism? What relation can in fact be conceived between the two, and what is the nature of the 'between'? Let us take a step further in exploring this point. Either one or the other, in fact—the two camps have a long-standing split. The first option is to consider generosity and egoism as completely antithetical, forming an antinomical couple. Not only can the one not proceed from the other but also it excludes it by setting off from an origin opposed to it (Good/Evil); their 'between' is then one of (the most distant) antipodes and calls for an incompatibility of principle veering towards Manichaeism—and, in fact, this is really the solution given by metaphysics as is seeks only to 'ground' (*fond*) the most ordinary moral and socially utilitarian position, the one congealed as 'common sense'.

Suppose, on the contrary, we use our ingenuity to show, as a subtle psychologist would, that generosity leads us without difficulty back to egoism— -that it is fundamentally only a more refined avatar of it. Just as the classical age was content to show that pity does not emerge from the logic of an interested calculation, it will be said that one acts for others to benefit oneself (and we do so without even having to project ourselves into the future, hoping that some deferment might intervene). Suppressing any distance between opposites, in this case the *between* is then effaced and the one is reduced to the other. There is no paradox in this, the moralist will say against facile moralization: If I so generously take an interest in you, it is to retain my expansive vitality, to keep myself busy, especially so as to devote myself to something in order not to waste away by withdrawing into myself; to give of myself benefits me directly. Who does not see that the Little Sister of the poor is radiant and has no need to wait for Heaven in order to be rewarded? It is easy to state that such an opening to the other acts to promote myself, that my generosity is self-gratifying and that this devotion pays off immediately—I have a presentiment that my survival is at stake (and therefore it will be still more to my advantage) to surmount my immediate advantage (a ruse of Life as it is of Reason). It is a question of the same interest—'egoism'—but in the shorter term, more profitable and better conceived.

Touching on the first thesis, Nietzsche has said it all: the impermeability imposed by morality between these oppositions is artificial—a true cloak. On the contrary, we ceaselessly have to uproot it for it is perpetually attached to the defensive force that this position secretes equal to its denial. But would this for all that invalidate the opposing thesis? This thinks it is de-mystificatory and does not mean to be the dupe, but is it not also superficial, notwithstanding the 'depth' of introspection it demands? Not that its 'pessimism' penalizes it (causing it to declare it 'unliveable'), but I believe it stops too soon along the path. In being content with leading one back under the other and in suppressing the *intervening period*, does it not tip over into an inverse forcing, a shielding that is just as fraudulent even if not so lazy? Admittedly, generosity towards the other benefits oneself, this much we are aware of, but for all that is this to be confused with self-love? Are we not allowing ourselves to fall into the trap of a too-easy inversion (denunciation)? For generosity *at once* connects up with the grounds of self-love *while* opening up an opposing direction for it. This is because, in the economy of forces, generosity is simply a more elaborated, more refined (and more hypocritical) version of egocentrism—it also turns back against itself, contradicts it, and, extending in an inverse sense, finds its energy in this refusal.

To think through this *between* egoism and generosity, maintaining the latter intense, letting it neither strain nor atrophy, neither seal nor efface, means, therefore, refusing the facilities of exclusion (through an incompatibility of essences) as well as those of confusion (leading back to the identity of one of the terms) in order to reveal how the two effectively communicate in their ground(s) while highlighting their differences in an extremely effective way. This is to understand what makes its fundamental ambiguity but also what this isolates in the way of (properly moral) choice, such as to allow it to orient itself in both directions, thereby restoring a possible connecting up—here Hercules finds a crossroads and can have a choice between the contrary parties.

If I am so kind, it is because I also know how to be cruel and the same faculty of personal investment will be drawn upon for each. This is so to the point that whoever does not know how to be cruel will no longer be able to be kind—the two (kindness–cruelty) draw their possibility from the same well, are cut from the same cloth, but their opposition is not for all that simply measured in consequences alone. It will instead be necessary to hold each at once under thought in order to think through life—their fundamental *unity* (and nothing, in fact, is closer to kindness than cruelty) at the same time as their capacity to *diverge*, and the tension they open: the latter is what constitutes the dimension *deploying life* (as a fan valorizing possibilities). And this is not because they maintain such an affinity between themselves, to the point that it undoes their identity, that the conflict between them would be illusory.

But how could we name this fundamental of the *between* or of the ambiguity that can result in the one as well as the other, since its mark is to hide all demarcation, its characteristic is to abolish the exclusion of the characteristic? What name should be given to that by which (more radical) opposites are found to be complicit with each other but which is itself nothing but these opposites and does not render their opposition artificial? What name should be given to the play, or the *connecting* that is essential to life, which is not constituted by a (hypostatized, metaphysical) third term nor allows itself to be absorbed into the finality of a dialectical overcoming? Which would keep the oppositions open to each other, even untie one from the other, but without cutting the extremities away from them? Heraclitus named that commonality of correlated opposites 'God': 'God is day night, war peace, winter summer, satiety hunger' (Fragment 67). A return to this elementary issue of hunger and satiety alternating like day and night, or war and peace or the seasons: not so much, this time, in order to evoke the transition from one to the other as to reveal the possibility which causes them to communicate from within—precisely what Plato refused to think about—and through which one tips into its opposite. In this way it is not in isolating one from the other, says Heraclitus, by raising antinomies, that we 'understand' God, but in 'taking' one 'with' the other—such is 'com-prehension': hunger with satiety, day with night, and so on.

To consider such a formula as simply signalling towards the identity of contraries, as we ordinarily interpret it, and as making opposites appear in their unity, is, I believe, still partial and too abstract; it especially does not allow us to understand what follows (correcting as little as possible), that '(God) is differentiated (like fire) which, when mingled with scents, is named according to the aroma each emits'. 'God' serves not simply as a way of saying that opposites are indissociable, that one cannot be taken without the other (neither the day without the night nor life without death) and that it would be both superficial and arbitrary, or, rather, once again a denial, not to recognize the dependency which causes them to proceed one from the other and that intimately links them. But this comparison still inclines us to understand something else, and this is something which, I believe, is even more precious—that, just as fire assumes one or another aroma, this common ground ('God') is manifested (is recognized and 'named') either as one or the other, offering itself equally, available as it is, to one or the other possibility; and that this divergence, creating the *between*, extends the variety of the world, deploying life and creating its astonishing and immeasurable grandeur. This is why we call it *God*.

In fact, would this not be what is able to impassion thought most of all (both provoking and liberating it): What do we understand by 'God'? By following Heraclitus, we can expect from this question the whole elucidation of life, in a way that is sufficient and goes to the very heart of life, and therefore without the need for the intervention of any other level but itself. Such is the 'God' of Heraclitus that there is no further need to invoke belief. Is this not what, above all, needs to be thought, whether under the name of 'God' or something else, in order to rise to this ambiguous *between* of the undifferentiated— which is buried beneath the fragmentations of language, in withdrawal and hidden, but from which opposites constantly emerge? If we are to cease to allow ourselves to be obsessed by one contrary to the detriment of the other, unilaterally affixing desire to it (whether the 'day' or 'summer', whether 'peace' or 'satiety'... seen each time as the better side of things), it must be acknowledged that the discrete on this side, which is the link to the other, has to be discerned so as to rise to the intense *between* which holds them in correlation. For all that, if it is necessary to return to this side of the antinomies, it is not in order complacently to reconcile them but, rather, equally to reveal and keep open how each of their possibilities, just as they communicate in their foundation fond with their opposite, is affirmed and develops fully—how it promotes life through its divergence.

Let us consider by application, from that point, whatever vital distinction you want, singular and typified. From there let us, for our part, forge our tool to analyse life. But this will be an analysis of a new type, one which neither separates nor 'challenges' one in relation to the other, as is traditionally required by 'analysis', but illuminates one through the other (since they undo themselves one from the other at the source) while keeping them opposed. How thus to approach the 'anxiety of those who are daring' (*die Angst des Verwegenen*)? For it will not accept being immobilized in a diametrical opposition to 'joy' or 'comfortable enjoyment' (of an 'activity which will peaceably go from before' as Heidegger said [1998: 38]). This antithetical blockage, by being isolated in its essence, would enclose it in our intelligence. For, 'on this side of these oppositions', it maintains a secret alliance with its opposite that will be better understood in its richness, not only *against* but also *from* it—even if this would be only the 'serenity' and the 'sweetness of a creative nostalgia'...

Or let us consider what causes the Greek *pharmakon* to emerge in an exemplary way which refers (as much to one as to the other) to a 'remedy' or 'poison'. This double participation in one as in the other then brings us back to the common element, a 'medium of every possible dissociation' (Derrida 1981). If the *pharmakon* is 'ambivalent', as Derrida says, it is really in order to constitute the 'medium' (or, let us say, the *between*) in which the oppositions are thereby opposed, 'the movement and the play which links them among themselves', 'reverses' them and causes them to pass from one into the other (this is the '*differance* of the difference'; see ibid.): holding in reserve 'in its undecided shadow and vigil . . . the opposites and differends that the process of discrimination will come to carve out' (ibid.).

8

I nonetheless wonder: Is this strictly speaking a question of 'ambivalence'? While *ambivalence* expresses the simultaneous coexistence of oppositions (at once I love and detest an object), the *funds of ambiguity* is such that the one opposed is not yet distinguished from its other; the separation between them remains indecisive. The ambivalence arises again from the perspective of the platonic mix impelled to the point of contradiction and does not bring back into question the identity of each of the contraries—their dualism remains justified. The components, both positive and negative, are mingled in the same subject but they are still differentiated from, even to the point of violence. Evidence is provided by what was already the 'ambivalence' of love and hate in Freud (according to that invaluable term borrowed from Bleuler): 'hatred' finds its origin in the drives of self-conservation and 'love' in sexual drives—one like the other has its own source or ground (or life drives / death drives). The *ambiguity*, in contrast, is traced back to that hidden point which it is so dangerous to confront through thought, and in which the one communicates deviously with its other and reveals their *joint* being. In so doing it dismantles their essence. Similarly, by way of consequence, it is here a question less of 'reversal' (of one into the other) than of a *fluctuation* tipping, from the ambiguous *between*, from one or the other side—deploying almost indifferently one or the other possibility. But, of course, everything is held in this 'almost'. . . .

What therefore is this 'moment', understood here moreover no longer in the physical rather than in the properly temporal sense, that is so slender and discreet but also the most fascinating we have to live, in which we could equally easily tip into one as into the other, into love or hate, desire or disgust? Not that, this time, disgust results from a reversal born of repletion-satisfaction, as in the idea we have of it which has been worked even in the imagination of paradise, but because there suddenly emerges, and in an indecent way, their secret kinship—the veil that conceals their ambiguity is finally torn. Sade's intelligence, in his paroxystic narrative, was to break through in the moment at which what I experience in such a violent way or, rather, as taken to an extreme, would not at the same time and in a contradictory way be both desire and disgust, but could equally well tip over in one direction as in the other, into desire and disgust, suddenly revealing to us, in this passage to the extreme, their disturbing complicity. In this respect, what remains of a properly ethical subject? When it comes to Her, it is not that at the same time I love and hate her, which in itself is not a problem, except at the risk of schizophrenia, since it does not once more bring into question what I understand *a contrario* as one or the other; but I equally experience that strange moment when, in the overflowing turmoil, I can just as well do one thing or the other—welcome her or leave her. Henceforth, this will no longer allow itself to be reduced to psychological categories, as we take so much delight in doing so as to be rid of it, but allow an insolent truth to intrude—it makes us notice, we the terrified, a possible (limited) point of *equivalence* between these opposites.

Hence the necessity to refuse the one as well as the other: *toughening difference*, as classical ontology does (Aristotle: to go 'from difference to difference' to the point of 'ultimate difference' unveils our essence); as also *denying differences*, with everything becoming equivalent (the sceptical position which withdraws from any possible engagement with action as with thought). The end point is not even to relativize the differences in order to find a happy medium between the two but to do both things—to return to the indifferentiation of differences to that extreme point of equivalence and tipping over from which their ambiguity comes, as well as to accompany the slightest difference as it moves forward, in its development, so as not to lose what intensity it may bring by contrast. In all, this means to open up the virtue of the *between* in both senses—that of the *link* by which the one joins the other (in those grounds in which they undo their identity) and that of the *divergence* and the tension valorizing, the one by the other, the oppositions that emerge.

Living, in other words, in the sense of promoting life, will conjointly imply two things, and it is in this respect that living is strategic. On the one hand, not losing sight of this (downstream) point of coincidence of oppositions, in which one communicates internally with its other, in this fundamental *between* of ambiguity—which would avoid letting ourselves become obsessed by one or the other, in neglecting the extent to which they are interdependent. But *equally*, on the other hand, of choosing (a moral or poetic choice) to develop one rather than the other and committing oneself all the more resolutely in a direction that we know for the other, loitering behind, having not for all that vanished. This would be at once to neutralize the incompatibilities in order to release the resources lost in these disjunctions *and* to activate the differences in order to carry the field of the possible further forward (to open it more broadly). Satiety will then no longer need to be feared, turning to disappointment, life then developing its values more diversely just as, according to the spices thrown into it, the fire or the God of Heraclitus exudes its scent so distinctively.

9

The Chinese have not, as did Heraclitus, called the *foundations of ambiguity* 'God' but have conceived it in relation to the *tao*, the 'way'. The *Laozi* poses it at the beginning, and in relation to the most matricial couple of all, under whatever slant one envisages it— that of the 'there is' (actualized) and the 'there is not' (of the undifferentiated funds); or of the 'named' and the 'nameless' of the (manifest) 'beginning' and the 'Mother' (of Origin), of the more 'spread out' and the more 'subtle', or again of the state of 'desire' and of that of 'non-desire' (§1):

The two have the same origin but bear different names;
that they have different names is what is called unfathomable;
unfathomable and still more unfathomable,
such is the door of the throng of indefinitely suc-cessful arrivals (or: infinite subtleties)

Right away the correlation of the groundless ground of latency (of immanence) *and* the endless actualization of differences (of existences), of the unnameable (indiscernible) quality of the undifferentiated and the demarcation through the word distinguishing the oppositions in it, is indicated but not justified because it is held to be the regulation or the respiration of the world—and not as a principle, some *arché* from which thought would begin to be constructed. There is no possible beginning of an ontology, the path to which is barred from the start, because no standards of being are established. What is grasped, instead, in a global apprehension, is the continuous communication between the common (non-actualized) before and what follows of the actualization (diversity), or from the *springing up* to the *settling down*, this process of life having no other horizon except itself in its inextinguishable ('unfathomable') capacity to renew itself.

It is logical, from that point, for the *Laozi* to invite us to com-prehend as Heraclitus does (that is, to take opposites together), since they pass from one to the other, as from the 'beautiful' to the 'ugly' or the 'good' in the 'non-good', since they proceed one from the other, and above all between the 'there is' (of actualization) and the 'there is not' (of the undifferentiated: *you wu xiang sheng*, §2). 'Beautiful and ugly are like joy and anger', indicates the commentator (Wang Bi); 'Good and not good are like true/false (positive/negative). Joy and anger have the same stump, true/false (positive/negative) pass through the same door; this is why they cannot be considered separately, by setting up one to the detriment of the other.' And again: 'All these contraries equally open up a natural arrival,' he continues, which 'hardly needs to be said' and due to this fact is legitimate by proceeding *sua sponte*. This is why one cannot fix them as antinomies, including at the level of values. The disjunction and the exclusion of opposites, as fundamental to the *logos* as to morality, are consequently considered to be uncertain, and the Taoist thinker teaches us to withdraw from them:

> *Agreement and disagreement,*
> *By how much are they to be separated?*
> *Good and evil,*

By how much are they to be separated?

(*Laozi*: §20)

The demarcation between contraries becoming hypothetical, the indecisive reappearing in them, the *between* is no longer one of separation but of communication, and Chinese thought will not have to go back against itself, as the European has to, in order to make its place in this joining. Consequently, with no map of Being definitively compelling the separations to be marked, there is no further need to work in return, against the grain, in order to detach the notion of 'ambiguity' from it after the event. It is implicitly admitted and constitutes part of the tacit understanding of life. In China, literature has no need to compensate for philosophy.

Nevertheless, the concern of the thinker of the *tao* is really to hold both at once, without rejecting, in the name of common foundations of ambiguity, the differences in the illusory and the artificial. On the one hand, the *tao* 'communicates as one', as is said in the *Zhuangzi* (*dao tong wei yi*; Guo 1983: Chapter 2): leading to going up to the common fundamentals of opposites, whether it is a question of a wisp of straw or a large pillar, of an ugly woman or the beautiful Xi Shi; indeed, of everything that is, 'strange, curious, bizarre and even monstrous', the *tao* reveals their fundamental 'equivalence' (such is the notion-title of the chapter). On the other hand, if these contraries are not made to 'serve' in a disjunctive and antinomic way (*wei shi bu yong*), whoever aspires to wisdom 'does not any the less take them into use' (*zu zhu yong*) and does not for all that renounce their advantage.

An apologue is thereby recounted which reveals at once the radicalism of the indifference and the good circumstantial use of the slightest difference. A monkey breeder distributes chestnuts to them, saying 'three in the morning and four in the evening', and all the monkeys became angry. 'Well, then, how about four in the morning and three in the evening', and all the monkeys were content. In one case as in the other, the 'equality' of the two situations is well respected, Zhuangzi comments, at the same time as the master of the monkeys knew how to take advantage of the simplest modification (*between* evening and morning) to go from anger to joy. He knew how to maintain the fundamental equivalence, which serves as a backdrop to life, at the same time as taking support from a slight variation in order to find a way out of the situation, to redeploy in this way the possible and re-engage life. Life is fundamentally 'equal', letting its equivocal nature be foreseen; but it extends (is enhanced) through the divergence one can deploy in it. To such a point that a trifle can overturn every-thing; the tiniest thing, a nuance, can effectively change the world.

IV

TO ENTER INTO A PHILOSOPHY OF LIVING

1

In the spring of 1756, upon leaving Paris, the salons and the 'Holbachian coterie',[7] Rousseau settled down in the Hermitage. After so much time spent in the hurly-burly of the capital, it was important to recover the sunken lanes and undergrowth, even just a little bit of garden where the earth could be scraped—he had lost all that since the blessed time he spent in Les Charmettes. It was by walking among the thickets and fields, he confides to us, and not in the confined atmosphere of a room, that he succeeded in writing. Is not such the influence of the environment on our capacities? He then inspected the works he had in preparation (at the beginning of *Confessions*, Book 9): *Political Institutions* (from which he would develop

The Social Contract), manuscripts of the abbé de Saint-Pierre to be put into shape, as well as a third work whose idea he owed, he tells us, to observations made about himself and that he felt he had all the more energy to undertake because he anticipated that the book would be 'really useful for people' and 'even one of the most useful that could be offered to them'. What would he therefore deal with in this book?

Could a book not be created out of the remarks one makes in this way over the course of the days about how objects and our external surroundings influence us to the point of modifying our behaviour and even of our way of existing? Would that be so negligible? It was a matter, on a grand scale, not only of things like climates or seasons but also of specific sounds and colours, the noise and the silence which surrounds us, the darkness as well as the light, rest or movement, and so on, 'everything' *via* our senses and organs, 'acts on our machine and soul'. Even changing the food we eat changes us—who has not noticed the fact? Everything offers us in this way a 'thousand prizes . . . to govern in their origin' these feelings of which ordinarily 'we allow ourselves to dominate'. So many *things to grasp*, Rousseau tells us, allowing us to establish an 'external regime' which would best condition the internal economy of our being—the concept

of it is therefore more strategic than properly moral—
it gives a signal towards a concerted management of
'living' that we could establish not so much thanks to
the traditional apparatus of commandments, prohi-
bitions and prescriptions, as by an attentive deduction
of the effects of everything which, unknown to us,
can affect us from outside and form our *ethos*. Was
Rousseau, moreover, not in the process of experiencing
this that spring, by moving from the city to the country and by going from streets to sunken lanes, from
the tumult to the silence, or even by eating once again
the fruits of the orchard just outside his front door?

Rousseau found a title for this book and even a
subtitle (*Sensitive Morality* or *the Materialism of the
Sage*). He flung the sketch of it down on paper and it
seemed easy to him to form it into a book that would
be as 'agreeable to read as it was to compose'. He
confesses that he then did hardly any work on it and
in the end did not write it. 'Distractions' prevented
him. . . . But why is it precisely this book, which it
would be so easy, and useful, to do, that he did not
write? The observations on which it rested are nevertheless, he assures us, 'beyond all dispute'. Why from
then on this abandonment? I wonder if he did not
keep to the very object of this book or, rather, to its
object/non-object. Certainly the comments are rich,

the observations are beyond suspicion, and it is enough to allow experience to speak, but the question is: How, in the matter of 'living', to go beyond this state of simple observation or comment?

The problem is that once he resorted to Locke's sensualism to give the controlling idea of this enquiry its philosophical armature, justifying in this way the passage from the 'physical' to the 'moral', how could an argument be constructed in such a way as to go beyond the anecdotal on the one hand while avoiding tipping, on the other, into arbitrary systematizations (in fact, Rousseau would deal with these comments and observations one by one in the course of his work)? Even when he evokes this principal theme of the work, Rousseau visibly distorts it. Giving way to facility, he reinvests his subject with sermonizing and traditional moral discourse (to 'make us better', he justifies himself, not to 'succumb, and so on); and he does not sufficiently free himself from the stake he nevertheless reveals. How can this be conceived without deviating (into the rut of pleasant feelings that has already been traced)? Did not this work, which promised to be so easy to write, turn out to be the most difficult?

In order to recognize this difficulty, it is necessary to divulge the divergence in play between 'living' and 'life'. Life easily lends itself to discourse because it is apprehended at the stage of representation, which is also that of objectification, and is conceived at various levels. It receives determinations that are perceived from outside—beginning and end, birth and death. It is understood in senses that can be separated—the biological sense ('all the functions which resist death', Bichat said[8]) or the ethical sense; a general or individual sense (*A life* is, for so many novels, the generic title of this singular); a characteristic or figurative sense (the 'life' of a people, literary 'life'). Taking into account this distribution of levels which, as such, are operative, one can elaborate knowledge about life and each of them possesses its pertinence and its object. But where is the verb going, or what has the noun already arranged and rendered analysable, which the verb holds as inseparable? For 'living' does not allow dissociation into various levels, nor does it authorize exteriority; upon it no backwards step is possible. Have we not been committed to this 'living', isolated and without landmarks, ever since what is always, for each of us, the dawn of time, and without our being able simply to imagine that it could ever be otherwise? We are unable to conceive of not living. Because 'to live', in the infinitive, is that anonymous nominal which right away withdraws all support of difference, whether of subjects or conjugation, from thought, and only retains its activity; but in so continual and discreet a way that we do not experience it as activity. Living is that eternal silence, implied right within us without our understanding it. How can we get a 'grasp' on it?

Likewise, we cannot develop from the outset a thought of 'living', as we do of life or anything else, but it is first of all necessary to 'enter' into it. *To enter* demands passing from an outside to an inside and requires a deliberated change of position. Indeed, it calls for participation: to enter into the affairs of someone, into his feelings or ideas, announces that one is beginning to open up to them and implicitly to adhere to them. *To enter* therefore involves a shift in two ways: its goes past a speculative level to an engagement while implying a resolute displacement of the self-subject, without which there is no access. The fact that we need to 'enter' into a thought of 'living' is therefore an intimation that it cannot be found directly through the ordinary enterprise of thought, whose work is to construct. This is why we notice that such a thought of 'living' does not conveniently become the object of a book, remaining in the undeveloped state of remarks and observations, and this is so even for someone who remains convinced that he would be the best person to pursue reflection about it—the author of *Heloise*, the *Confessions* and the *Reveries* (and let's not forget *Emile*: 'Living is the profession 1 want to learn'). This is why it has remained, all the stronger for it not being admitted, at odds with the characteristic project of philosophy. This meant that philosophy soon abandoned it, to the extent of forgetting it or throwing it into a sort of childhood and, let us say, a stammering of thought.

2

In fact, what philosophy in Greece did, in a masterly way, was to make us forget what living is, and this is why we need once again to return to it in order to measure its incidence. Does not this 'well known' remain unknown to us, so strongly did we assimilate it long ago? By sharpening (at least since Parmenides) the principle of non-contradiction (but living being grasped only on this side of such an exigency) and by posing from the outset the idea that 'wisdom' (traditionally bearing on living) is identified with 'science'— *sophia* with *épistémé* (at the beginning of *Theaetetus*: 145e)—as well as considering (on the first page of the *Metaphysics*) that there could be no wisdom or science in the elementary expression of 'living' that is 'sensation', of *sophia* in the *aesthesis*, philosophy committed itself to the adventure of *logos*, as a demonstrative and determinative discourse of knowledge, and has taken 'truth' for its objective. 'Living', as a result, escapes it.

Philosophy has dropped living because it is too embarrassing (and too inconvenient) for what it wanted to undertake, which was nothing less than to elaborate a literal, and therefore abstract, level on which thought could operate as it pleased. In raising an absolute metaphysic, like the Idea of the Good in the platonic *Politeia*, the 'cause' at once 'of science and truth', on this clear foundation, that of 'Being', all-conquering philosophy would no longer allow 'living' to be apprehended in its plenitude and according to its logic (a logic decreed as illogical) except in the shadow or under the overhang of its own edification, therefore in a depressing loss in relation to it. The consequences can be measured—it has been necessary to put this apparently incoherent living in care, *by way of* morality. In the same way, living is no longer recognized in its eminently *relational* content but henceforth rejected as being *relative*.

We can read this more closely in what Plato presents to us after the event as a parenthesis, or as an 'hors-d'oeuvre' (*parergon*, at the very heart of *Theaetetus*: 175c–177a), but in forthrightly summarizing how the future of European consciousness will be marked with his stamp in an indelible way, with a

red-hot iron, I will abandon from the outset the relational (of the type: 'What wrong I do you or you do
me?'), as Socrates tells us, 'in order to examine', by
detaching myself from this individual, 'justice or injus-
tice in itself', taken in their essence or 'generally'
(*holôs*), which means in a way which would no longer
be relative but absolute. Admittedly I would not be
very good at everyday activities, at installing a travelling
rug or seasoning a meal, but only I could sing 'the true
life of the blessed gods and mortals'. A passage
solemnly occurs here from 'living' to 'life' with the
latter aligned over it and, moreover, demanding to be
referred to the 'truth'. What does 'true life' (*bios
alethes*) mean here, though? Plato leaves hardly any
doubt about how it should be understood. It will be
opposed to 'that place', which necessarily remains
haunted by evil, that 'over there' from which it is necessary 'to flee' as fast as possible in order to 'assimilate
oneself as much as possible' with the divinity. It will
mutually separate two models, or two 'paradigms': one
that is 'divine and blessed', and the other that is 'the
most unfortunate and atheist', because atheist, and we
will be punished by this very life, as miserable as it is,
that we then live. This theme of 'true life' will now
endlessly project its shadow over 'living' and darken
it to the point of closing access to it, and it will
unexpectedly pass, even if their conception of God

might be very different, into patrology (from Philon to Clément or Gregory of Nysse), which is why the Church Fathers have reclaimed Plato.

Likewise, what needs to be retained from Nietzsche, when confronted with 'Socrates', will not so much be the 'affirmation' of life against its negation or the 'yes' spoken to 'ascendant' life against exhausted life—this cry of Dionysian jubilation comes only after, elevated as it is a little too theatrically against all resentment and enjoying its prodigious fecundity to the point of sacrifice. It will, first, be necessary to retain this, which precedes the judgement of values and becomes a method (counter-method): that philosophy must return to the 'living' it has occulted; or that we have made no 'other representation' of 'Being' itself, as Nietzsche retorted, than 'the fact of living' (1968a: 3.§582). Or, again: 'Being is only the generalization of the concept of living' (*leben*) (1968a: §581), that is, he immediately makes clear so as to avoid any abstract deviation, principally of 'respiring' (*atmen*). What access, indeed, could we have to 'Being' if not through the elementary form of 'living', but which we find covered over, crushed under the 'question of Being', and which therefore makes it necessary for us to extricate, against the current of the whole of this history, from underneath the construction of thought?

Henceforth, what is important is this—while 'Being' thinks itself according to the categories that have been forged in order to grasp it (of 'identity', 'substance', the rupture between reality and 'appearance' and consequently also of 'truth'), 'living' will be rediscovered only through a retreat from those predicates which have dominated metaphysics and by 'reversing' them. This means not only thinking about mobility against the immutable, as has been said so often, or about ambiguity against essence, as I have started doing, both of which are then no longer signs of lack or deficiency, but more still, or more generally, in thinking about the 'innocence' of a 'living' liberated from all external recuperation and submission to ends. Better than the ideologically suspect theme of 'health' or the facile denunciation of values forged by Decadence, *innocence* (*Unschuld*) is the powerful concept which expresses, in Nietzschean terms, the fact that 'living' does not allow itself to be aligned with anything, does not allow itself to be measured by anything, does not refer to anything other than itself, has no goal but is valued only in its own terms—it does not demand to be legitimated. Any meaning you like can be given to life, but 'living' is definitively *outside meaning*. Why therefore go to so much trouble to recognize it? Moreover, living is no more mysterious than it is absurd; but living finds its justification only within itself or, rather, it enters into no justificatory plan—'living' has no way of justifying itself. This is really why philosophy turns away from it and is even intent upon concealing it. Having no 'hold' over it, it has constructed its monument to 'true life'.

3

At the heart of classical philosophy, thinking about 'living' likewise appears only in the margins or *aside* from it, remaining in a state of observation and remarks. Consider Descartes, in some of his letters: just try to imitate those who 'when looking at the greenness of a wood, the colours of a flower or the flight of a bird' allow their attention to drift and 'convince themselves they are thinking about nothing'. To release this internal tension which eats into her (and so distresses her), Descartes suggests that the princess should transfer her gaze, at will, onto the slightest manifestation of spontaneity as of the variety of the living which surrounds her—to which she belongs. Make the pure (naked) feeling of living, as phenomenal and organic as it is, well up in you again, in order to release her from her preoccupations and experience them indifferently in nature. Descartes stopped here: if 'living' re-emerges in this way in thought, it is only in passing, even once more flowing into morality, even if the latter would rather be about hygiene, and one is left with the familiar mode of advice (letter to Elisabeth, 1645). Descartes says nothing more about *living* itself. In the same way, on the first page of the *Critique of Judgement*, Kant really postpones the sensation of satisfaction (faced with the beautiful) to that 'feeling one experiences of being alive', but says no more about it. He gives a signal further on, but just in passing, towards some such phenomena of promotion or of 'intensification' 'of the entire life of humanity' through pleasure; but, having perceived it, he does not embark upon this path (1978: §1, §54). For he had interests elsewhere, preoccupied as he was with regulating the internal play of the faculties of knowledge and conferring an anthropological status on finality. 'True life' still remains on the horizon.

Would this not be the backdrop of all reflection, which we know is extended at the back of any topic? But the only thing we know what to do with it (alas!) is to conceal it? Otherwise, would not this 'living' be understood as the stubborn silence from which all philosophical discussion momentarily (sporadically but noisily) detaches itself? Not only does Plato himself abound in remarks about living, as soon as he takes a break from metaphysical construction, but he also places on stage, and in a noble way, we should acknowledge, the very ones which refuse to allow themselves to be fascinated by it. In any case, he knows how to hold us for a precious moment in the complicity of living, on this side of the perilous decision of philosophizing, openly revealing its threshold, the leap it entails and what it makes us move on from. The old man Cephalus (at the beginning of the *The Republic*) goes off to attend to higher tasks when the discussion about justice takes a conceptual and constructive turn, leaving behind experience—he abandons the concern to make the effort to the younger people. In the *Philebus*, hardly has the title character indicated with a single sentence the primacy he accords to pleasure than he then says nothing more about it. He stays, but withdraws from the debate (Protarchus is supposed to represent him, but we can see what a struggle this second role is). Philebus remains present, but is silent. Does not his silence alone express enough about it? It incarnates 'living', and his tacit apprehension weighs more heavily from that point on than all the arguments put forward. Such a silence is, moreover, neither religious (faced with what the followers of Aphrodite would consider the ineffable quality of pleasure) nor disdainful. But, for Philebus, this debate, by wanting to place meaning

and construction where it is not required, is meaning-
less. He watches, amazed and perhaps amused, at the
other debaters around him as they strive. But how
disconnected they are from 'living'.

Similarly, Montaigne assumed to himself alone,
and in a royal way, this entire *margin* of philosophy.
In this respect, he must surely have remained unique
and without genuine descendents. For he was not
hesitant about making 'living' the principal stake in
his rationale, which is gradually uncovered until his
work walks more and more surely towards it. In the
final essay, 'About Experience', this theme, although
it is not at all a 'theme' (living has no particular content), ends by dominating all others and taking them
into its embrace. Did he even have any other theme?
At the end of such a gradual process, Montaigne
exclaims simply that: 'Our great and glorious master-
piece is to live in a timely way'—a virtue of the infinitive. He even makes audible the absolute in this usage,
to which nothing need be added: 'I have done nothing
today—What? Have you not lived?' Does this 'lived'
not immediately shut us up because it contains everything? Is it not a response to everything? Does it not
bear within itself its own justification—its sufficient
satisfaction? Is it not its own destination? It designates the horizon of all plenitude that careful thinking

would vainly like to go beyond. Indeed, Montaigne makes a powerful notion of this infinitive to which all things return, which he takes a delight in substantivizing, but of which it would be useless to gloss and whose content is too absorbing, pregnant, entire, to be made explicit: 'As the possession of living is shorter, it is necessary for me to render it more profound and full' (1987).

This unique title, this title as strange as it is simple, *Essays*,[9] a title as strange as it is familiar, which has established a line but whose audacious plural for ever preserves it from being copied, is really the only one which could advance such thinking about living, allowing its emergence without already starting to exceed it, without right away causing it to deviate into some orientation or destination which would assign and stiffen it, in short, without damaging it. 'Essay' is in this sense open, but it especially intimates, according to this 'living', that everything remains in process, that no conclusion is to be anticipated, no ending to be projected, and that the test prevails over the conclusion. 'Essay' draws right away, discreetly but with authority, the thought, whether it is alarming or reassuring, of the End. For who could make 'essays', he forewarns us, 'who could not know how to create effects'? An 'essay', in other words, signals towards *springing up* and not what settles; expresses not the determinative but the *conative* (*Conatus* has been one of the ways of translating this title into Latin). A possibility is attempted each time but without there being any fascination for the limit, or haste to go beyond.

Thus there is nothing in the 'most extreme old stories', Montaigne remarks, that 'we do not try every day'—our quotidian living, we know, is richer than our imagination. 'To try' means to experiment but by being revealed gradually, as it tests but without forcing, assuredly in a concerted way but which keeps something improvised and which is reflected upon as it advances, avoiding the definitive. When we 'try', we decide in an incontinent way what fits, according to the evidence, as we try on clothes or taste a wine, making each time the first time, without projecting a shadow over it or prejudicing the outcome—it therefore could not be further distanced from any sceptical position, an 'essay' is explorative and not disillusioned, and maintains in its freshness (its *innocence*) a continuous beginning.

We can write 'by way of trying' (as La Boétie did in his youth, according to Montaigne) but also 'the whole of this mess I scrawl here' is only a 'register' of 'essays of my life'. For what can one do except *live*, when one does not illuminate it by the End? One cannot explain it, properly speaking (all causality quickly becoming exhausted in it), still less construct from it (unless one wants to protect oneself from it by this construction). We can only elucidate it from itself by 'registering' it, as Montaigne says, in its divergences and variations. Otherwise, in what becomes its sticking point and a covering over at the heart of the discourse, 'living' inevitably escapes. All one can say over and over of Montaigne's language and style, as he points out himself, is his originality. Ever since celebrated as an art of writing, it arises, in truth, only from what this 'inquisition' of 'living' has commanded—an enquiry of which the author is never tired and which really constitutes, this time, the connecting thread of a possible book (about 'living'), but the discontinuous and out-of-the-way character of which then becomes legitimate and is even openly demanded.

Does not Montaigne himself forewarn us that the reader who loses this thread is 'inattentive' and that his book 'is always one'? Is not the only way to grasp this unthematizable living through the digression which always comes back to it, proceeding more effectively by 'flight' than by 'continuing'? Is it not in the casualness of what never allows itself to thicken beyond the *remark*, but does not cease to return to the attack through another slant, 'loitering' and 'spinning here and there' and caring nothing for fashion? Only this continuous escape can prevent its escape. 'Mess', variegation and vagabondage, as also drawing upon speaking Gascon as in the gossip of fishwives, as well as making metaphors gush out inexhaustibly, tending less to cause an obstruction to the scholastic than, more essentially, generously to hold open all of the possibilities among which 'living' is called to renew itself; to maintain 'living' in its 'attempt'—breaking anything which creates a rut, contravening everything which scleroses and predisposes. In short, to 'let', as Montaigne said, 'the river flow under the bridge'.

No *constructed* clear, consistent and logical discourse can grasp 'living', as Montaigne perceived—this discourse can only erect 'Being' or 'true life'. It is, likewise, necessary to methodologically detach oneself from it, to un-mark and re-mark this living from every side, following it through an abrupt change of subject and into its various deployments, and thereby to thwart what all continuity would inevitably secrete of opacity in this regard. In this way is not 'living' 'expressing only half, expressing in a confused way, expressing discordantly'—all predicates contrary to the *logos* of ontology? Would this be a question of an elegance raising itself by means of its negligence, as has been so often said, of a nonchalant (slightly posed) unconstraint or a pre-baroque taste? Is it even the perpetual 'see-sawing' and instability of the affairs of the world that Montaigne has in mind? This is already too thematized. Might Montaigne therefore have been afraid of exhaustion? I would rather ask: Is it not a question here of the only possible strategy of bringing out our tacit 'possession of living'?

Taking advantage of the golden age which came only a little before that of the classical regularities, where usages had not yet been codified, Montaigne did not, he warned us, 'nail down' language but 'bent' it. Just as, in the pre-Cartesian era in which the identitarian system of the self-subject (*ego sum*) had not yet been accredited, he could depict himself as nuanced as well as 'formative'. For what is this 'I' that he paints? 'I do not paint existence but passage,' he warns us, 'not a passage from one age to another or, as the people say, from one seven-year period to the next, but from day to day, from minute to minute' (1987). This 'passage' does not express the flowing out of 'life' or 'time' in a banal way, in a retrospective regard equalling regret, on a more or less broad scale—the everlasting *topos* of the ephemeral and an easy *lamento*. Instead, he makes 'living' reappear in its

very *moment* or, as he expresses it, its occurrence—
springing up impromptu, 'essayed', drawn as it is from
what is implicit in it as also disengaged from what
ordinarily frames it, conceals and cushions it. Did not
Montaigne, moreover, avow to us, in confidence, that
he willingly awakens during the night in order to
experience it more keenly? On the subject of 'living',
will we ever emerge from the *private conversation*?

4

Montaigne chose to remain on the borders of philosophy, or in its *margin*, but philosophy, we see, has sev-
eral borders, and we must be careful not to confuse
them. For my part, I would distinguish at least three
of them in bringing into play in sequence these pre-
fixes: the *pre*, the *under* and the *infra*. Pre-philosophical
would designate what has not yet attained the philosophical and has remained in its infancy, in the state
of the wisdom of the early years. Its concept is notable
in Deleuze and allows him to arrange (perhaps too
hastily) traditions of thought external to Europe.
The *under-philosophical* would evoke, in an inverse
sense, what declines from philosophy and then tips
over into weak discourse, once more lazily becoming
opinion (it does not probe and is not consistent)
under the form of being popular, in which the effort

FRANÇOIS JULLIEN

of construction is lost. Today, thanks to the media, it has engulfed us—I'll say no more about it. By contrast, I would call that thought of 'living' that remains hidden and which we see emerge only in a Rousseau or a Montaigne as *infra-philosophical*. *Infra* does not mean an inferior level but what lies upstream and arises from what is implicit. *Infra* therefore signals towards what philosophy conceals, on which it constructs (in order to conceive of 'Being' or 'true life') but upon which it still depends as on a deposit or territory in which it takes root (according to the old metaphor of the 'tree' of philosophy). This ground into which its roots go thrusting is not for all that one of mystery or religion—the 'tacit' is not the 'ineffable'. Classical philosophy has not had a more cherished desire, we know, than to 'found itself', therefore from itself, therefore in placing itself 'first' and, consequently, of failing to appreciate this *infra* (of 'living'). So it is high time for us to realize that it can no longer delude itself with this illusion.

Nevertheless, what clearer line of demarcation can be established, even made tighter, between the *under* and the *infra*, that is, between Montaigne's subject and those of his imitators today (in the 'taste for living' category, that genre whose title itself says enough)? To invoke only a difference of quality (or of force, or inventiveness . . .) is insufficient. It can even be seen when the one is the most unlike the other in spite of the apparent relationship. Abandoning the exigency of the concept, and therefore the construction of the discourse, the *under-philosophical* spreads into common places and undeniably tips into preaching ('Deliver us from fears'). This 'us' of the pathos is artificial and vainly mimics simple thought—fortunately, philosophy does not 'preach'. In comparison, the defiance of Montaigne (or Rousseau) in relation to philosophy was, as I have said, strategic, since for them it was a question, by detaching themselves from the philosophical apparatus, of revealing this more elementary and fundamental living, which lies upstream from the constructions of thought but does not for all that get taken in by the old philosophical (ontological) myth of the underlying and the substance. If they each give the impression of talking about themselves, indeed, if they themselves express what they recount and 'depict themselves', it does not therefore mean they are interested in themselves, in spite of the facile *doxa* which has settled upon them, but because it is only in the meshes of such a 'self' that this *infra* of living, silent and imperceptible as it ordinarily is, and which moreover obliterates philosophy, can, as the evocation unwinds, let itself incidentally (obliquely) be captured. If the concern, in other words, is not with such a revealing, that of tracing back the living water of the depths of this well and procuring this understanding, we will once again inevitably tip over into false ease or sympathetic effusion, that of the under-philosophical, but now without a grain to grind, *flatus vacis*. As we have seen, even Bergson, when he treats *in fine* 'revitalization', 'reheating' and 'illuminating' life, does not avoid this facility (Bergson 1984).

Once this *distinguo* is operated, it is time for us to ask ourselves: Who has known how (been able) to treat 'living', gathered or, rather, 'registered', as Montaigne said, at the level of a phenomenological understanding we do not want to betray and without therefore allowing the concealing of the *infra* with constructions of Meaning and Truth? It is assuredly not the philosophy which makes an essence of everything it seizes upon, of 'Being' or 'true life', as Midas transforms everything he touches into gold, and whose task is usefully transferred elsewhere, into the production of knowledge, the one which has magnificently made the bed of science, and in the institution of policy. But neither can this be the religious message which, if it has promoted its *intimate* dimension, has from the outset oriented it towards eternal Life, in framing it in a *credo* while postponing it into a hope (*zôe aiônios*, according to Saint John: 'I am the way, the truth and the life'). Everyone will agree in saying that 'living' is what matters most of all to us, and yet. . . . Yet what place has therefore remained for us, in Europe, to welcome it, between science and religion, between the Progress of the one and the Salvation of the other, especially when the two intersect? Theology building itself into deductive knowledge and science into a new type of messianism? Must we abandon 'living' to primitive consciousness (that of the *pre-philosophical*)? Must we allow it to be buried (and therefore also dry up) under all the knowledges of life?

Likewise, we consider with disdain the springing up of 'personal development' *coaching* and all the rest today (not without reason); indeed, we are alarmed (understandably, of course) at seeing shelves in the bookshops of Europe full of a new vitalism, with its frankly inept content, proportionately reduce those of philosophy (I've noticed this in general bookshops in Hamburg and Milan as well as in Paris). In both cases, I fear, it will not be enough. In the same way, it is insufficient to record that faith in the Eternal, which until now has embedded our aspiration for living under true Life, hardly matters to us any longer, so much do we find ourselves increasingly reticent when faced with this great Postponement (into the Beyond) as with the dogmatic affirmation of some grand Narrative or unique *muthos*. Philosophy is therefore called upon to react in the face of this transformation which is soundlessly put into effect (that of our ideology), that is, silent but global, silent because global. It is finally obliged to come out of the woods, that is from the comfort of its history, in order to reconsider the traditional apportioning of discourses and roles, notably to think again its own condition of possibility, but just as much of necessity (or we could simply say of utility), for it too can disappear. . . . It can no longer remain, I would say, bolstered by the rationalism it incarnates and pretend, with crossed arms, to remain unaware of what threatens it.

It will therefore be necessary to begin by straightening out these rivalries, making a complete review of these pertinences. Philosophy is now invited to re-envisage the relation it maintains with its Other. Not only with its smaller others, like the sophistic or the rhetorical, which it reduced to silence or cleverly forced into obedience, or even with its great other, religion, its ostensible rival but also its secret ally, with whom the division of territories has long been arbitrated. It owes it especially in regard to that other inconvenient other, 'wisdom', for it is an other that is not other, having indefinable contours that are never confronted. Or philosophy believes (or pretends to believe) that it long ago dethroned and cast into a sort of archaism or quasi useless good sense the one whose very name is handed down to us like a vestige as pretentious as it is dilapidated. But 'wisdom', as disdained as it was magnified, does not for all that check out. From where does its force of obstinacy and resistance come? Is it not simply that wisdom has been alone in concerning itself with the 'living' which philosophy has abandoned? Is it not precisely because in it the pre-philosophical mixes equally with the *infra*? And even that, if one treats 'Montaigne's wisdom' inescapably, for want of another term and as a stopgap, it immediately has to be admitted that it arises exclusively from the second—from what remains ordinarily buried under the erection of discourse but has nothing for all that of having 'remained' (in some sort of infancy of thought)?

The fact that 'personal development' (the modern offshoot of this unthought) may be able to increase its market so easily today by means of non-books, and that it encounters no further resistance as it unpacks its exotic bazaar, is also a symptom of how much the territory between health and spirituality has been left undeveloped in Europe, and that in it thought about living has hardly found room to increase or, at least, to be acknowledged. Does not 'Montaigne' remain unclassifiable? We understand that philosophy can only protest by turning to this old and very vague term of 'wisdom', one lacking a proper notion, inconsistent and bloated, which hardly allows itself to be loosened from truism, hollowed out and no doubt effectively outdated. But, in order completely to do without 'wisdom', it would be necessary for philosophy to highlight its own relation to the *infra* and to consider how to become itself a philosophy as much of 'living' as of 'life', *Lebensphilosophie* as the German indifferently expresses it. If it does not want to vanish and if it wishes to retain its own tool, the concept, philosophy will even need to begin with this. It will need to start by more closely reconsidering the declared incompatibility, even open warfare, between what appear to be raised as very opposites: 'living', and 'concept'.

5

In the Germany of the Enlightenment, Jacobi is rather the odd man out. He was something of an auto-didact, did not hold a university post, started out by writing novels or, at least, what are conventionally considered as such, and principally composed letters and dialogues. He took advantage of his appearance, of his 'grasshopper' attitude (of a 'rhapsodist') and never produced any continuous treatise. Jacobi valued Pascal and Rousseau. He then made waves by reviving the question of Spinozaism considered as the culmination, by means of determinism, of a rationalist tradition which he showed had dangerously erected an obstacle against our apprehension of living and led to an existential strangling. What is most original about this position is that Jacobi did not cease to want, while demanding for himself a 'non-philosophy', to debate the point with Mendelssohn, Kant or Fichte, the philosophers of his time. He claimed at all costs to locate his thought of living, so resistant to concept, within the very heart of concepts (making of it a *Lebensphilosophie*). Likewise, he tried to give a notional content to what I call the *infra-philosophical*, and did so by showing how the knowledge constructed by reason is not always only 'second hand' but assumes an internal, anterior and first-hand certainty as primordial consent at once pre-reflexive and ante-predicative: it cannot spring up, we suspect, just on this side of the rupture between the subject and the object founding the operation of representation appropriate to knowledge. For, from 'living', he warns, who can in truth make themselves a 'representation' (Jacobi 2000), in other words, taking just a little distance in relation to it? Thus, for having neglected this undeniable fact, the European philosophical tradition unfortunately deviated, to the point of culminating, by losing the 'real' under the speculative, in 'nihilism' (letter to Fichte in ibid.). The end result, and the trial opened up against it, are contained in Jacobi. Did Nietzsche even suspect what he owed him?

Jacobi chose to call this *infra-philosophical*, in which the feeling of 'living' is apprehended, 'belief' (*Glaube*). But what is this term worth? Is it felicitous, or even just viable? Immediately, we need to separate it from that Faith by which Writing 'instructs' us, this elementary confidence, no longer *faith* but *belief* by which nature 'constrains' us—this is what causes us to enter into an immediate adhesion to the 'world', initially through our body, and without which we could not live. Such a term at least has the merit of emphasizing this common point—such a conviction does not await proofs and is not arguable, but is prior to all realization and touches upon existence itself. We have known since Kant, at least, that this is not one predicate among others and does not demonstrate itself (it cannot demand logical necessity, whether it is a question of the existence of God or of things outside us). When it comes to reason, it can only establish the relations between things. This means that it is necessary for things to be given before I can be in a position to perceive their relations—such is the measure of the *infra*.

So this belief, which from the outset gives us a guarantee of a 'reality' (which is why Jacobi claimed to be a 'realist'), as originary as it is unchallengeable, against which all fiction or methodological doubt in the manner of Descartes has striven in vain, which causes us invincibly to 'believe' that we are presently in this room and sitting at this table, constitutes the first 'element', or the middle, not only of all knowledge but also of the slightest possible activity. It is, in what it implicitly takes on, the pathway or, let us say, the initial, continually required, opening, by which 'living' is deployed and becomes effective within us (it thereby serves as a *Lebensverständnis*). Living is possible only through this *adherence* (to the *infra*) in which I am from the outset and that I do not question: 'Without belief, we could neither go through the door nor sit at the table or go to bed' (ibid.).

It is true that Jacobi fumbles as soon as he has set down this term of 'belief'. And, above all, in order to identify this prerequisite of the *infra*, is it better to envisage it from the perspective of 'sensation' or 'sentiment' (*Empfindung* or *Gefühl*)? The problem is that in the one case we will be cast among the sensualists while in the other we will be accused of exalted and confusing spiritualist sentimentalism, of *Schwärmerei*.[10] As we will inevitably fall under the axe of one or the other, it is necessary to begin by undoing this imposed bifurcation. But to turn towards what? Must anyone who wants to signal towards this upstream call it a *sentiment de l'Être* in order to avoid tipping over too soon into the order of representation or the reflexive? Or, in Kant's language, a 'transcendental aperception', in order to emphasize its unitary principle (preceding the data of intuition a priori)? 'Axiom' would be more common and convenient, but we also know that this is integral to the demonstrative discursivity from which it differentiates itself only by its quality of being indemonstrable; the 'pre-condition' (*Voraussetzung*) still belongs too much to logic (to the thetic). But is it not, from the opposite angle, too mystical to speak of 'injunction' ('of the true', *Weisung*)? Forged by centuries of the rationalism of knowledge, all these words, in terms of 'living', betray us. There will be no choice but to rework them as best we can, to re-cut their edges or go back to their etymology in order to deviate from their usage—in fact, to deviate from their deviation and thereby to understand them anew in *Vernunft*, triumphant 'reason', the *vernehmen* of a more originating perceptive, but one since then concealed and forgotten.

By oscillating from one to the other, although what he wanted to call attention to was not the interval any more than what is common to the two, but what underlies them, what is upstream or *infra*, Jacobi can only give the impression of a vacillation. A philosophical staggering—it really shows, they will say, that he was not a philosopher.... In fact he clutches a little too hastily at everything he comes across, clutching or rallying equally well to the radical empiricism of one (Hume and the evidence of the perceptible) as to the spiritualist ontology of the other (Leibniz and the 'de facto primitive truths' of a *cogito* Leibniz revised and corrected). But could Jacobi do otherwise? Could he do otherwise than clumsily trace back this *infra* of living to the surface of thought, above all of language, an act of adherence more than of actual knowledge but which centuries of philosophy have buried under their speculative edifice? Can one emerge from such a stammering to grasp this continuing *springing up* of living which, at the same time and in the same movement, *entrusts* us to some world, falling short of our categorizations? At the beginning of *The Visible and the Invisible*, Merleau-Ponty hesitates in the same way and has difficulty finding the right expression. He too was unable do otherwise than evoke a 'perceptual faith' which is 'common to the natural man and the philosopher—the moment he opens his eyes'. For does it not postpone it 'to a deep-seated set of mute "opinions" implicated in our lives'? (1968). And Merleau-Ponty adds in the margin: 'Notion of faith to be specified. It is not faith in the sense of decision but in the sense of what is before any position and . . .' (ibid.). An uncompleted or even, more strictly speaking, uncompletable note—because how could it be developed?

Was Jacobi therefore wrong in wanting to accommodate the tacit evidence we hold about 'living', implicated in it and certifying itself there without possible or, from the outset, 'convincing' argument, at the heart of a philosophical panoply whose first ambition—that of the 'Enlightenment thinkers'—was precisely, as we know, to draw everything into the light and hunt down the implicit? Was this not contradictory? For he said himself: Such a 'sentiment' (of 'living') can only recount itself. Did he therefore not need to remain at this level of concerted recording, but by its continuous variation ('attempted') eluding the interruption of the concept, on which Montaigne prudently settled? Was not Jacobi's enterprise condemned in advance? It has to be admitted that his thrusts, disordered as they were, had consequences, that they even produced an astonishing effect—they caused upset. Fichte promised repeatedly to respond to the *Letter* in which Jacobi challenged him, but never did. It is very difficult to refute someone who has himself come out of the play of refutation.

Likewise, taking precautions against what he perceived in Jacobi as the threat of irrationalism, Kant had to undertake nothing less than the long detour of the third *Critique*, in going beyond the two others. More precisely, he needed to do two things at once: to conceive of a rationality of a new type, since it no longer extended to knowledge (that of 'reflecting' judgement), while making fresh use of what is no less a concept, even if one that is different from all others (not being one of understanding), that of 'finality', once again, the founding of a new (and ultimate?) teleology of Creation. But in so doing Kant tips back into the thinking of life, even of 'true life', extending from the causal order of nature to the 'reign of ends' emerging from all that is conditioned and with man as its 'final end'— 'living', occurring and not dependent, *innocent* as it is, once again escapes him. In the same way, Hegel produced one of his most powerful theoretical efforts against Jacobi, resulting in the central thesis of his whole system and claiming to regulate once and for all the dispute appearing between life and the concept—far from life being external to the concept, it is the concept which will contain the very structure of life.

6

It might be thought that, by daring to put forward this thesis, in other words, by carrying the rationalist temptation to an extreme, Hegel can only lead us further away from 'living' and inevitably cause it to become lost in abstraction. Nevertheless, the question arises, and we are not going to be hasty about cutting it short. What can this Hegelian elaboration of the concept of life (or the life of the concept) bring to the elucidation of living insofar as it is the case that Hegel not only recognized its eminently *contradictory* character but also devoted himself to unfolding it? It has been said, and repeated so often, that 'living' eludes the light of reason because 'living' demands a place within contradiction, whereas reason excludes it. By legitimating contradiction at the heart of the concept, from which he drew its development, did Hegel also burst open the exclusion between living and the concept? Consequently, we no longer hold on to the facile partition according to which, confronted with Hegelian universality through the concept, the adverse option alone, that which promotes the *individual* and is so resistant to the concept, which from Jacobi extends to Nietzsche or to Kierkegaard—all of them being heralds (heroes) of the Singular—can contribute to the elucidation of 'living'. As we know, Hegel all the same demanded such 'concretization'.

If it is true that every given concept (every cut and dried concept), even one of finality, which is nevertheless the most buoyant, can only be pinned onto 'living', it is no less the case that a philosophy of 'living' will be able to develop only at the heart of a tension or a conceptual polarity. Otherwise, the elucidation of *living* by philosophy would have to be definitively abandoned, since its tools are judged as inappropriate. And, in such a case, the position of a Montaigne, settling himself resolutely on the margins of philosophy, would without doubt be unsustainable; and the clumsy (the ill at ease) Jacobi could only serve as proof *a contrario* of this failure. But, as soon as philosophy, by itself introducing contradiction into the heart of the concept, so radically re-elaborates its means of operating, as Hegel in fact does, the question is no longer settled in advance—against a whole narrated history, Hegel (the Hegel of the *Phenomenology of the Spirit*) was, I believe, the first philosopher who tried to restore the thought of 'living' into the heart of philosophy.

'Living', as we have acknowledged, means to pass into its other, *to de-coincide* with itself and constantly to elude itself; it therefore follows that it undoes the principle of identity, itself the founder of the principle of non-contradiction. Let us then think of life between these poles: between what Hegel called the *unity* (or, according to his terms, the 'infinity substance' or the 'fluent continuity' or the 'in-itself', or the universal fluid medium, or the capacity to 'keep oneself equal to oneself' and so on. See Chapter IV, Section 171 in Hegel 1977); and, in opposition, the *scission* (that is to say, 'individuality', the 'for-itself', the various 'members', the 'autonomous forms' and so on). Let us thereby place face to face this plural facing this singular. From where can the *movement* of life and its continuous alteration come between them? We understand what makes life be life, equal to life, in its continual springing forth, as Hegel advances, as soon as we take account that each of the two terms, whatever they would be, instead of being blocked within itself, reveals 'just as much the other' (*aber . . . ebenso*, serves here, by its systematic return, as a logical articulation). Thus, the 'for-itself' of the independent forms is equally immediately its other, their 'reflection' in unity is equally the 'scission' in these forms which each keeps for itself.

To take a closer grip on this movement developed in moments, for here 'movement' and 'moment' recover their etymology and coincide anew: if the 'simple universal fluidity' is the 'in-itself' and the difference of 'forms' is the other, this 'in-itself' of the fluidity in its turn equally becomes, through the differences, the other. *Equally*. . . . That the one is revealed equally to be its contrary, this is the real 'Revelation', and the one could not expect anything else; and that it would therefore be called to turn back into itself in order to be able to become itself is what of itself *sets in motion*—the movement inherent to life. Thereby the unilateral quality in which knowledge (that of 'understanding') is fixed becomes undone; by the same token, the one overflows the frontiers of essence, enclosed in its determinations, under which the thought of 'living' until then had been lost.

What makes life be life, passing restlessly into its other, is that, as soon as thought separates its two sides, as Hegel shows, each does not remain within itself, nor remain in the self (*à soi*) but time 'place' its other in itself; and they, consequently, continuously exchange their determinations between themselves, suppressing them at the same time as they conserve them and thereby going beyond themselves in this movement (that of the *Aufheben*). In this way, if a first moment would be that of the various forms holding themselves for themselves and seceding from the unitary substance, this moment is by the same token the 'repression' (*Unterdrückung*) of what has come before, that is, the other that it also is (that of such differences 'having no persistence as self in this universal medium'). Likewise, a second moment necessarily follows which is the 'subjugation' that comes (*Unterwerfung*) from such a maintenance of differences under its other—that 'infinity' of the difference it has repressed and which will ceaselessly renew itself, in dissolving forms and altering itself without respite in this unitary process that is life.

Admittedly, this claim to submit life to the dialectic has entailed a well-known indictment: 'There cannot be,' retorted Kierkegaard, 'a system of existence in it.' Then again, it will be conceded, the deployment of such an infinite movement occurring of itself can be valid for a course envisaged in its generality and regularity, mimicking the laws of nature and what lies beyond consciousness—only here is this abstraction valid, which has to be weighed down with some materiality to be useful in History. But what could be illuminated by this machinery, by this play of negations and their reversal, of individual, personal and always inchoate 'living', of a subject constantly projecting itself ahead of itself and each time clearing a way for another possible adventure, in short, ceaselessly *trying its hand*? What could be clarified, in other words, by what has since been called (and precisely against Hegel) by that word expressing so much unpredictability—Existence?

I would rather believe the opposite. There is less to take from the Hegelian conception of life as universal flux, whose 'circle' is systematically accomplished in opposed moments and by 'turning on its axis'. But to have conceived that the reversal of one into the other is likewise due to that very fact of a reversal within oneself (*Verkehrtheit*, which equally means misinterpretation and absurdity, and not simply *Verkehrung*), in other words, to have introduced contradiction as the driving, and not the deficient, element of living as such, *das Leben als lebendiges*, is the lesson to be gathered, and, above all, concerning the subject and its intimate development, something all the more advantageous as from the beginning it does not pull towards morality.

This is what, at least if I in this way cut the sequence out of it and unhook it from the inevitability into which Hegel allowed himself to be caught up, does justice to a sublation by alteration stemming from the impossibility of remaining there (*Unruhe*), which carries forward, and invents a new present through dissatisfaction with any state, experienced as immediately mortal. Would not 'living' be defined, in fact, in going back to Hegel, as the unacceptability of contenting oneself with that point, whatever it might be, or of remaining (resting) within oneself? Therefore as passing into one's other in order to be self, or 'making oneself become other to oneself', as is said when the contradiction is grasped (*sichanderswerden*). For life to be conceived as that whole 'developing itself' and 'dissolving its development' and 'conserving itself simply in this movement', as Hegel concludes, is what portrays 'living' in the enduring capacity of emergence that it finds within itself—in its continual revival, or its *springing up*, without there yet being Meaning to draw us forward or *telos* to project.

On the other hand, that life would be 'itself at rest while being absolutely restless infinitude' (Section 169 in Hegel 1977) no longer separates rest and movement into two opposed worlds or realms, as classical ideology had done until that point. Remember Pascal: the movement of 'agitation' on the one hand and 'Heaven' on the other, the rest towards which the soul aspires. But here movement and rest finally cross, and are made to 'fall one into the other' (*ineinander fallen*) so as to form the internal tension that is 'living' and constantly instigating. And this more than anything is what Hegel brings us. It is true that there is no concept that gives us the satisfaction of thinking about 'living'. But as soon as a concept, any concept, is itself no longer satisfied with itself, but itself makes an appeal to its other, it can finally grasp 'living' and no longer play on an open string: since living already means to pass into one's other. If 'living' cannot illuminate itself from *a* concept, which could persuade us of the irremediable incapacity of the concept and make us abandon the attempt to grasp 'living' philosophically, condemning us to a non-philosophy, it is, nevertheless, in the play opened by two concepts which contradict one another, as one beats two flints together, that 'living' is finally illuminated. And that a *philosophy of living* can begin.

7

Likewise, to enter into a philosophy of living not only relates to the displacement that this initial work operated step by step—the necessity of thinking about *the moment* as it is occurring, springing up, contrary to the equalized and planned time of metaphysics, or such that it is devalued by 'falling' outside the Eternal (*supra*, Chapter 1); either to think about the *springing up* in the face of the settling, or the effective over-flowing all determination in the face of its lapse into a flat evidence which means one no longer perceives the latter, which can only be revealed by its withdrawal (Chapter 2); or to think about the *between* and not the end, the tension in process which makes it relate and not the temptation of a term or projected meaning (Chapter 3). If we are to enter a philosophy of living, is it not necessary, at the same time and in a parallel way, to tie up each of these terms that are set off against their opposites? Would this thereby be without interruption to make contradiction express itself by disclosing them?

This is renewed in stages. In this way to refrain from a *postponement* so as not to let the occasion which is offered be spoiled at the same time as to know how to *defer* so as to allow the favourable moment to ripen of itself (1); or to give *coincidence* and *non-coincidence* their chance at the same time, being careful to support it with evidence but to open it up to the abysmal ground-less, and to discern an inherent property of living in this depropriation (2); or to go back into the *undifferentiated* of differences up to their extreme point of ambiguity, equivalence and shaking, at the same time as to accompany the slightest *difference* in its development so as not to lose what intensity, by contrast, the latter can bring (3). It is necessary to hold the two conjointly—neither to sharpen their confrontation into a paradox nor to take it apart into an alternative but to remain just at that point of tension where the one requires its contrary in order not to allow itself to be enclosed in itself and to miss 'living' through the resulting unilateralism and rigidity.

Once this illuminating moment of contradiction is grasped, the only way of procuring an internal day and expecting nothing from an external Light or Revelation, 'living' will allow itself to be caught in the net which all of these oppositions weave. Living is not external to the concept, but overflows from any reduction to a concept which *stops it unilaterally*. This could be stated otherwise—each of these concepts turns out to be pertinent if one does not lose sight of the fact that its contrary is equally pertinent, and that it is from the way they are tightly serried together, which on each occasion is unique, that the coherence which *maintains in life* can emerge. Let us go back to the highest of them, which the eviction of their other, having sometimes been neglected, has fossilized. It might thereby be doubted whether *immanence* (or equally *transcendence*) would still be useful, still encourage thought, because this antagonism has fixed and sterilized them so much that the one immediately awakens the suspicion of the other in the museum of philosophy. But, instead of maintaining them in a mutual exclusion, 'living' is understood precisely at the juncture of the two (*infra*, 1). Or *normality* is no longer false, in terms of 'living', if we know how to open it, at once to activate and compensate it, by what I will call, in opposition to it, *deviance* (2). Even *knowledge* recaptures all of its rights in order to define our relation of those living in the world if we reveal its *connivance*, in comparison, as this contrary from which it detaches itself, but from which it does not for all that cut itself off (3). In following these lines of tension one after the other, a philosophical grid of 'living' can begin.

This is the banality of our modernity, but it is not exhausted—against all assigned transcendence, a thought of living is conquered, or is torn, only by a resolute affirmation of its immanence: *immanence* is that polemical concept which has liberated life. 'Living' is envisaged as such, or becomes conscious of itself, only if it is understood, in other words, if we stop being afraid of recognizing, that 'living' proceeds only from itself, is not reliant on anything else, nor has any need to invoke an external cause or support; therefore it does not cause any other level to intervene, therefore no 'plan' properly speaking intervenes;

or—as the Greek already expressed, but in a way that is very difficult to bring out of its abstraction—has its 'principle within itself' (*enuparchon*). A cause that one believes to be understood, at least when it is quickly expressed, the philosophical conquering of the religious, and this trial is no longer to be enacted. All the transcendence we put aside, or simply separate, overhangs 'living' and hides it.

But for all that, *transcendence* does not delegitimize itself. Its notion cannot be emptied out, not because of its metaphysical residue but because 'living' does not support this univocity—its self-deployment is understood only as also being promotion and surpassing. As soon as transcendence is not constituted externally to the process engaged, is no longer of the order of the level but of the activity, then immanence itself is affirmed only as it leads to transcendence. We already know this from biological life which is continuously transcending both its structures and its performances—sickness and degeneration are the loss of this 'audacity' leading us towards further exceeding. It is especially due to this that human 'living', extracting itself by virtue of 'existence' from natural life, is in a position to describe itself by its capacity not to remain within itself, to dis-adhere from its state, to overcome the limit and to project itself—to *emerge*.

Nietzsche, who did so much to free immanence by denouncing the illusion of ideal worlds, did not renounce this transcendence. The abandonment of the 'Beyond' is not found at the beyond of oneself: to vanquish and surmount oneself (*überwinden* responding to the Hegelian *aufheben*). 'I am that which must overcome itself again and again' (1961: 138), he makes Life say in *Zarathustra*. Indeed, the more one is resolved to free oneself from the transcendence which comes to us from enacted morality, the more need there is to impose an internal discipline on oneself, so as to elevate oneself from the self, in other words, from its own capacity—the whole of Nietzsche resides in this equation. The less we accept authority, the more necessary it becomes to *create* oneself from out of the demands one gives to oneself. It should be understood that such an overcoming is to be considered as turning finality inside out—this transcendence is deployed in an immanent way or, more accurately, deploys its capacity of immanence, translating itself into a 'force', only if it tends towards nothing other than to jog vitality from its rut so as to lead it to transgress its limit and, in confronting itself, to 'sublimate itself' (*sich sublimieren* is actually the Nietzschean term): the merit of the over-man, the artist of himself, is to be able to do this by going beyond the fiction of a goal. In order to avoid a drift into a new mythology (the one which threatened Nietzsche) this can (and must) be read phenomenologically and as being ordinary (and not as a separate experience, even one of anguish—see Heidegger 1998). For the 'going beyond' or 'outside' that is characteristic of this transcendence (*hinausgehen*, as Heidegger says) is included in the very structure of humanity's 'being-there'; and this forms its subjectivity by maintaining it precisely in this emergence (Heidegger 1965). Likewise, this 'towards' (*zu*) of the opening towards which people are borne, far from conducting them to some Elsewhere or separated Beyond, is that of gaining access to what is 'in the midst' of the world.

8

One concept necessarily calls upon its other, in terms of 'living', so that it can lead it out of the unilaterality into which it would otherwise be condemned to fall—in order to keep it from exercising a monopoly which immediately becomes reductive; the reduction, in such a case, is precisely nothing other than death. If we understand it in this way, *normality*, according to the *Littré* medical dictionary, as the fact of leaning neither to one side nor to the other but of holding oneself upright in the happy medium, such a normality corresponds to the equilibrium of life, logically finding its negative and, because of this, its exclusive opposite, in *deviance*. But is this the case with 'living'? Why should such normality, which already corresponds to a medium and is essentially functional, be reserved for health? Canguilhem points out to us that the sickness within us also assumes its norms, as it takes up its quarters, even if these would in fact be vitally inferior. Likewise, deviance, logically contrary to such normality, does not for all that lead to pathology. What we learn especially from Canguilhem is how to distinguish such normality, established by means of statistics, that of a course which has become customary, from *normativity* which for its part is an aptitude to produce norms; and he especially reminds us that, in opposition to physical or chemical phenomena, which are axiologically indifferent, biological life is a phenomenon which is always preferentially oriented ('polarized', as Canguilhem puts it) and already lies between injection and dejection (between food and excrement)—it constantly separates within itself what is propulsive, or *instigating*, carrying it forward in a positive way, and its repulsive (negative) contrary: 'Living means, even for an amoeba, to prefer and exclude' (Canguilhem 1991).

How then not to see, from that point, that such *deviance*, in contradicting the *normal*, can, through its dissidence, be what reactivates the normality that is led to enclose itself and subside into its own ordinary course, to lose consciousness of itself and renounce its normative activity—to waste away? Hence *collapse* threatens 'living' in a surreptitious way. This deviance then once more renders normality inventive and instigating, by forcing it to react, and, consequently, to respond to the exigency of the normativity of what is vital and so plays in favour of dynamic polarity—it maintains 'living' as a springing up or in its emergence. This is a concept which then becomes as much ethical as biological—it even takes such a separation apart to its advantage—at least as long as this deviance is distinguished from deviation, so that it knows how to preserve the virtual, the new and the novel within it and not sink into an actualization which freezes, by repeating itself, and reifies it in a new *habitus*; that this other possibility it opens up is in fact kept open and not blocked. This is because, as soon as it normalizes itself, deviation too becomes a rut and then permanently enclosed in the pathological.

Reading so many diaries of artists and writers, following indiscreetly all the confidences they murmur, or even if this would first mean opening libertine literature, we entertain no further doubt about the way in which such deviance cooperates with 'living'—

it re-incites by counterbalancing a normality which has become deadened, causing the normative to rediscover the vigour which, instead of flowing into (of lying down in) the normal, is recharged against it as an offensive value and even finds itself becoming inventive. Nevertheless, judging from so many confessions, their naivety is often amazing. Is it feigned? One of them recounts his evening in a seedy place as though there was nothing to hesitate about this fact even though everything in it sufficiently revealed the opposite—that it was Desire, sharpened by perversion, which led him there. No, this *divergence* (of behaviour) is aimed at something other which is not ordinarily said: Is it not above all to shake him from an existential torpor and awaken him from that apathy which threatens (to disentangle 'living')? We cannot be satisfied with what is currently reported, and about which the confidante himself so willingly deceives himself—that he acts in this way only to purge drives or to free himself through licence; or by means of the sexual to free himself from the spiritual, or to touch the obscene so as to emerge refreshed. . . . No, these propose, rather, nothing but pretexts. And, in the same way, when we claim to open, through debauchery, a safety valve in the effort of creation, some compensation for ascetic life, all the more aberrant in that this effort is absorbing; or simply to give in to the fascination of pleasure. Or to replay the everlasting scene of temptation and provoke Satan—to defy the conventions of morality and signal an artistic behaviour. Or to yield to this brief 'descent into hell' so as to open up the human compasses more widely and get to know other useful experiences as material.

What is hidden under this eccentricity that is more embarrassing than the whole mythology of the bohemian or accursed Life, the pose of defiance or even a concession given to depravation, because it then eludes the conventional play of morality and its subversion? Is it not to stop far too soon to be satisfied with the old challenge to habit made to justify this voluntary derangement? As we shake the dust from the carpet, it is a matter of clearing away the vitality, by this jerk, from what has gradually been deposited in it, blunting its edge (its energy) and deadening it— 'living' suddenly shakes itself from its disintegration. As it does so, this open *deviance* tests again less the silent and regular norm of the normal than the more ambitious one of the normative—it effects a clear grasp of the separation between the two. It is really the current normality of my life which ends up obscuring this normative capacity. In other words, this deviance leads momentarily towards placing our normality at risk in order that, by playing with fire, the normativity of the vital is once more rendered effective; above all, it restores the polarity more vividly, by suddenly making us flee anew by means of this negative surge from the situation and in this way proceeding objectively and coercively (even though it is a question of a self-subject allowing itself to be thrown into confusion) into an internal de- and re-structuring.

This occasion is therefore not one of dissipation but of reactivation—it newly brings to light and causes the re-emergence, as a possible choice, of something whose legitimacy was no longer perceived under lassitude. It is a matter, therefore, of the ruses of Deviance as of those of Reason; and whoever says rule says strategy, which separates us from morality. They lead us to interpret that which in fact arises from a logic of 'living' but which no longer finds in Art or the festivity something to satisfy it, as an appeal of pleasure, one all the more seductive for being associated with the forbidden—in it an upsurge of vitality is produced, even if through disgust. Under the form of Desire, what is depicted is a means of restoring time in tension and coming out of its *settled* course. This logic is harsher to recognize in its economy than it is to confess pleasure by means of one's prank.

Canguilhem did not hide the reticence that all vitalism inevitably provokes; yet it still did not disappear: 'The vitality of vitalism,' he wrote (2006). It has to be admitted that its mechanistic contrary, although assuring its positions still more solidly, does not manage to evacuate it. From where, then, does this capacity of resistance come? Vitalism, for all that it tries in vain to be no more convincing than all indeterminism, makes an appeal to notions that are irremediably vague and not justifiable from the scientific point of view (the *impetum faciens* or 'vital principle', and so on); it even regularly takes up service again next to the most reactionary ideologies, one once more and perpetually resorts to it. One has recourse to it, instead of getting rid of it, not for the knowledge it brings but for what it produces of *a necessary reopening* or disclosure—in order to prevent its (mechanistic) opposite from sinking into a partiality which consists, as we say of it, of 'explaining life without life'. Confronted with its reduction by this causalist explanation, 'living' involves an appeal to a concept of 'exuberance' that goes beyond the norm, with which *deviance*, due to this fact, shares common ground. Did Nietzsche himself mean anything different when he evoked the 'charm' of evil in regard to all 'land which is exhausted', his force of stimulation or this leaven of the real which is the negative? (see *The Gay Science* [1974]: 1, §4) What the purely reactive morality of the 'good' defuses of transcendence, comes back to the joyful (and generous) affirmation of the 'bad' so as to 'rekindle' it—they are the 'useful' ones. . . . A suspect vitalism once again, but one which is of value due to what it recalls, here from the point of view of a collective living and which can be political—that normality, without deviance, itself ends in deviation and that it must have recourse to its other, not through tolerance but by tearing itself from itself in order to advance.

9

Between *knowledge* (*connaissance*) and *connivance*, the connecting is different again. For man, 'living' is deployed through the activity of knowledge which, developing as speculative knowing (*savoir*), will turn against the need for adaptation from which it is born and want to make a break with it—knowing which henceforth tries to be 'for knowing' or pure knowing, taking itself as an end and claiming to be disinterested. Such a knowledge is disconnected from what is vital. It dissociates itself from what I call by opposition *connivance*, knowing that remains tacit, which barely reflects or explains itself and, by tenacious coupling, is maintained in an intimate relation. If the contrary of knowledge is ignorance, its contradiction is this connivance—*connivere,* to understand with a wink (see Jullien 2006).

Knowledge isolates a 'nature' and places it as an object, methodologically organizes its progression, elaborates its tools of abstraction, produces notions and constructs mediations, renders spaces indifferent and projects an equal and mapped out time; it develops an argued discourse which promotes the conditions of science as well as politics. But can this be the *totality* of knowing? Does 'living' not assume a mode of intelligence or, more accurately, of 'understanding', which, weaving itself as the days go by, even without our thinking about it, without our thinking about thinking about it, holds back in adherence (instead placing at a distance)? Is not knowledge simply the illuminated face that is only made possible by the connivance of its reverse which backs on to it? A shadowy knowing which remains integrated in an environment, does not abstract itself from a landscape, is not extracted from a conditioning, does not separate theory from practice, does not detach a 'self' from the world and remains on this side of any possible exposition—to know, in other words, the *infra.* Precisely what Jacobi inappropriately called *belief.*

The *connivance* is this knowing of the *infra* and the implicit which has not broken its attachment. The child on the breast or in the lap of its mother still has practically only this sort of knowing. Then, with schooling, with the equalized settling imposed by writing and the distribution of knowing into disciplines, objects are delineated and isolated, maps divide up what reason should link—this connived knowing (*savoir*) is covered over as soon as a knowledgeable subject conquers its autonomy. It is also this connived knowing, which is moreover excessively complex when considered from outside, that anthropologists find in cultures that have remained primitive: a knowing in which the senses and the intelligence are not dissociated, where it is activity which comprehends, each limb that discovers; where prudence is queen and vigilance its path of acquisition; where man remains actively involved in his environment and finds everywhere around him partners with whom to communicate silently—with the mountains and the waters, with the dead; with animals and spirits and plants. Man hoards them at the heart of a collective memory but does not mark himself in a History; he links alternating moments but does not construct a projected Future. Connivance came to him from his living in unison (with the elements, the ages and the seasons);

in other words, from the fact that the world still exists for him as *springing up* and vibration. Knowing or, rather, relation-knowing, which does not adventurously explore an Outside but enfolds itself in an Inside, is a native knowing of the native; and its language remains a dialect which does not come up against translation. An old parallel: as the pupil must make a break with his childhood, civilization buried this connivant knowing and lost it. Or, rather, it has always already disavowed it, and its nostalgia for such a connecting onto the immanence of the vital still runs underneath the monuments erected by knowledge.

Do not two lovers *live* together in or, rather, *through* a relation which is made of connivance more than knowledge? Do they not spend the whole day speaking to each other without saying anything which could be kept as a record? 'Have you seen?', 'I know that . . .'. Under the banality of the exchange, they rekindle an agreement as they breathe: this wink of the eye is the entire day—'amorous babble', as Rousseau said. I even wonder if the whole of social life (in the family, in groups and even in business) does not assume a lot more connivance than we believe (that is, of knowing about the *infra*)—words which teach nothing and even aim at nothing but which maintain a relation of adherence, folding over the sphere of exchange 'in the middle' and allowing understanding to filter through, more than that they communicate real information.

Or, again, is not poetry in its entirety (when it is not simply discourse in verse and responds to its vocation) a word of connivance, reconnecting us to the immanence of the vital, which favours a whole play of internal understanding and adherence (images, rhymes or assonances)? Or, that in deploying such an echo chamber, the word folds into it in connivance. Overall, poetry reverses the relation and causes the human to backtrack. As opposed to knowledge which breaks with connivance, the poetic word detaches itself from the discourse of knowledge and effects a return to the 'primitive'—it integrates and reconnects, reintroducing us into the state of common vibration or of *springing up*. Do we not need to become connivant again in order to read a poem?

What I am trying to say is that the vine grower maintains a relation of connivant knowing with his vine—he needs to take account of so many factors and degrees which knowledge knowing would be unable to go through and analyse. The (a) 'profession' is learnt but hardly taught; it is the fruit of routine and past time, resting on an un-said of understanding more than on explanation and demonstration, hence the difficulty of transmitting it. I deduce from this that there are two ways of 'grasping' when it comes to our work and our enterprises: the first is connivant and seeks the 'oblique' (as the French speak of the 'biais du gars'[11]); while the other acquires knowledge and orders through method. In order to survive in society, has it not been necessary for me to learn in a connivant way, through silent recording and at the level of experience, what I have never been told and which may even be the reverse of everything I have so often been told? Indeed, are we not all placed in a connivance of the human, as far as 'living' is concerned, which has never been completely made explicit, in spite of a millennia of literature but which means that we understand what has been murmured about our condition, palliating in this way its want of sufficient reason? Whenever I go on holiday or for a walk, 'recharge my batteries', go into a forest, I retrocede within myself, taking myself back to this latent accord and knowing—in relation to the waves, the meadows and the trees—and once again become connivant, knowing what I was. Does living not consist of alternating one and the other—of rendering myself more knowledgeable and connivant according to the moment? I rely on the one or the other touch;

I proceed (into knowledge) or retrocede (into connivance). Who could ever have taught me this behaviour by alternation and its art of variation? It brings to light, in any case, once more, that 'living', caught between the two, arises more from a strategic comportment than from morality.

V

THE TRANSPARENCY OF THE MORNING

1

This leads us on to another question. It will no longer be the classical question, and even the question par excellence, reshuffled in every way as cards are reshuffled: How should life be conducted? The Greeks already posed (*pôs bioteon*) such a question. A moral question, that of the right *or* wrong path, of the road which goes up or goes down. As though this layout of the paths was not already part of the *settling* and that the question of choosing them, even though they have already been signposted, could conceal the (prerequisite) one of *access*. Access to what if not to 'living'? Does anyone who has before then gained access to living still need to ask questions about good and evil, or about right and wrong choices which from that point appear so abstract and artificial? Also, how would it be possible to gain access to 'living' if 'living' is our immediacy?

How to *gain access* to what or in what we find ourselves already still committed—from which all springing up and plenitude originates but which is precisely what we lose hold of because we are immersed in it? What cannot be captured—there is always the problem of the 'grasp'. What obliqueness, ruse or detour could be introduced to enable us to lift ourselves to the point of facing that from which we remain ineluctably without a distance which allows us to conquer it? By what means (or mediation) can we arrive at living if it is our immediacy at the same time as it contains every possibility, that it is the foundation and the source, but that it is an immediacy to which we cannot gain access? In addition—if we were actually to gain access to 'living', we would no longer have to ask ourselves 'how' to live. If I therefore consider that 'living' is a strategic concept, rather than one arising from morality, it is because living has to do with an achievement (a harnessing) and is the consequence of conditions, being of the order of results. It is a question of getting round an immoveable difficulty, a matter, as they say, not of 'values' but of success and failure, but a success which certainly has nothing to do with 'succeeding in one's life', the selling point of under-philosophy.

The first and most radical solution, to introduce a distance that would once again allow us to reach this, the one Plato kept to, is to effect a *division into two*. To do this is, as they say, to separate 'true life' from living. It is to renounce the immediacy of *living*, as ungraspable as it appears, by detaching from it what it raised of a 'beyond', *meta* (the *meta* of metaphysics), which would finally be 'stable' (*bebaios*) and might serve as an 'aim' (*skopos*). If *living* is that immediacy which, due to this fact, does not allow the distance needed to conquer it, the convenient thing would be to dissociate from it the veritable life (the *alethes bios*) projected at the level of Being or the absolute and from which the evanescent living of the here and now is no longer anything more than a pale 'image', a reflection struck with loss. 'Living' is brutally cut in two: this life here is 'in a dream'; that life over there (*là-bas*) is the only one that is 'awake'—it is the only reality. This life here, in its immediacy, is inconstantly-inconsistent: purely metabolic, it is limited to the fastidious repetition of the same; condemned to mark time, it cannot possibly progress. That life there, at a distance and which effectively imparts to us the path, even the limitlessness, to be taken, is the one towards which, as travellers impatient to arrive at port (*The Republic*: VI–VII), we can from now on ardently walk.

As we know, Plato took an axe to all this. Not because he was disgusted with living, as might be suspected, or because he was directed by some obscure resentment or sickly aversion, but in a logical way—when one is entangled in something, it is necessary to know how to restore some separation (*chorismos*) and this calls for the courage of great surgical operations during which hesitation would be very dangerous. Are we not tired of living in the twilight and half-measures without having—knowing—what we can use to guide us? Or of only being able to count on an inherited morality? From 'living', which is phenomenal and so diverse, ambiguous, contingent, inconsistent, inchoative, incoherent, and which has still only been sketched or 'tried', let us draw up a 'true life' whose unitary essence would definitively be solid since it is the product of the concept and derives the perenniality of the thinkable from it—it alone can be founded on principles, and finally 'touch' upon 'being' while all of a sudden breaking with appearances. Let us 'pose' the latter as the goal of the other—let us operate methodically, therefore, through abstraction, in order to detach ourselves from this life here and through mediation, so as to cross the latter to have attained the other, thereby projecting a blessed life onto the horizon to which we would finally be able to gain access.

What is important is not so much whether we could raise ourselves to it (can we be so assimilated into the divine?), but whether an approach, and so above all an opening up, might be organized—whether a finality, thanks to this distancing, might become possible. Plato, in other words, sacrificed the immediacy of 'living' in order to develop its *condition of access*. The intellectualist 'in view of' of the Greeks (*eneka + gén*) is the great articulation which allows life to be structured in this way, by tearing it apart, all the 'existing' thereby most generally dividing into two: on the one hand, 'what is the aim' and, on the other, 'what is the aim of the aim' (*Philebus*: 53d–e). Now not only is the first inscribed in the dependency of the second but it also possesses value or consistency only through it—'living', buried in its development, the *genesis*, could only save itself by being sucked in by its destination.

The first sentence of the *Nicomachean Ethics* presents this, even if *a minima* and as a banality (at least, this is how for a long time I read it without lingering over it): 'Any method or investigation and similarly any action and choice apparently aims at some good . . .' Then one day we wonder: When he said this, was Aristotle having doubts about everything he assumed about choice? He puts it forward only as a résumé of common opinion and as a starting point from which to construct. But did he have any idea of the threshold he was crossing with this step towards living when aiming in this way from the outset at its surpassing? Did he see what option he had already taken in life by arranging it *from the point of departure* in terms of finality (that of the Greek *ephiesthai*, to be 'turned—extended—towards')? 'Living', as a result, straddles it—'living' is placed on the orbit of the Good and comes under the control of morality.

It will then be vain for us to distinguish between the various sorts of 'end', between those which consist in 'activities', those which are 'works' distinct from these activities, those between them which are subordinated and those which frame and cover them, with the end of ends, the 'sovereign good', *alias* 'happiness', at their summit—from that point, all of this changes nothing. Henceforth, true life is beyond, on the horizon, in sight, it is what is *after*; this After was what the religious soon seized upon in order to furnish it, but which Aristotle (even though he had little that was religious about him) himself began to implicate in the slightest aspect of our conduct. Consequently, true life is 'elsewhere', it is 'absent', and we live in the expectation of the End. As Aristotle had said: Is not everything 'vain' if we are without an end (the inevitable word, *mataios*. See *Metaphysics*: 994b;

Nicomachean Ethics: 1094a)? Take even something as simple as walking. The end of the walk, Aristotle will in the end say, as though it was obvious, lies in health; otherwise, this walking, which aims at nothing, serves nothing, 'is for nothing' (already stated in *Gorgias*: 468b). True life lies is in this Postponement.

Living is then experienced only through its contrary—if one seeks nothing *behind*; if one crosses the destination and it becomes contemporaneous with itself—if one refuses this convenience of throwing the quoit ahead of oneself so as to have to run after it. In short, only if the immediacy of 'living', as 'innocent' as it is, in other words, not yet having been finalized, is not abandoned—only if one walks, not for one's health or something else but in order to walk. Even this 'for', although it folds back into itself, is still too much: it is only if, through walking, that one walks—there is nothing to add. In Chinese, it can be very well expressed—the verb *you*, 'to advance' (as in *xiaoyaoyou*, the first and catchword of the *Zhuangzi*: to advance at one's ease, without destination, 'at will'). But how, then, inversely, not to allow 'living' to be absorbed by the immediacy in which we are immersed? For just as what is settled is no longer perceived due to the fact of its evidence, and requires a retreat in order to reappear, then living is experienced only if one is capable of detaching oneself from it, in one way or another, and causing it to re-emerge, so as to determine and *approach* it—a return therefore to the strategic question of *access*.

2

It is already true that wisdom has struck like a call to order against this postponement of living to 'true life', as well as the metaphysical construction which justi-fies it. It is addressed to us in a tone which is no longer demonstrative but familiar: 'You well know that living is in the end the only important thing. What does anything matter compared to its pleni-tude?' Or, if living has an aim, it is found only within itself; it is its own appropriate end and nothing must allow it to be divided in two or to postpone it—such is the Stoic idea of 'self-end'. 'Remember dying', *memento mori*, say the Platonists or the Christians as they call upon the hope of another life, the true life, that to which dying gives definitive access. Not at all, says wisdom (at any time, in any place) with its anonymous and, at the same time, unanimous voice, but 'remember living': *memento vivere. Gedanke zu leben*!—Goethe also made this his watchword; and once the word is spoken, everything is expressed. Or, in a still more familiar way, and like an adage, the adage being really the contrary of all construction: *primum vivere*, philosophize as much as you like. . . . Enough books, I want to live. When they are twenty years old, young girls in novels write it in capital letters on their bedroom walls and in their notebooks. They know it is the only lesson they need to keep, which they have not been taught and upon which they are relying in order not to let themselves be fooled.

But why is it always stated to us in the familiar tone of the motto or advice, indeed, most often of the aside? Why can 'that' (which matters most) never be constructed and developed? Yes, why is this 'in the end' always indicated only in passing, as though just a signal needs to be made towards its evidence? Why is it never argued against? As though it is enough to authorize oneself with the connivance into which we dip: Why is this 'in the end' never illuminated? It is an object only of instruction or exhortation, as though its value as a watchword was enough. Or, more conveniently still, it gives rise to denunciation, for then the counterpart is easy: 'There are people who do not live the present life', *ton paronta bion ou zôsin*, Antiphon[12] said before so many others: 'It is all as if they prepared themselves, by devoting their ardour to it, to live some other life . . .' Meanwhile 'time passes' (*chronos oichetai*, the Greek already states). Under the satire which begins, here we are soon made to return from it, once again, to the facility of morality.

At the very most, if there is theoretical effort, it consists in 'encircling' the present in which to live—it is only in this fold, wrinkling momentarily at the heart of an amorphous time, that living can let itself be gathered and captured. The Stoics learnt to 'limit' (*perigraphein*) this 'present' (*to paron*), the only real, actual, time—to sort out our representations attentively in order to separate from them everything which touches the future and the past, everything which is therefore of the order of fear or regret, which either does not yet concern us or is no longer our concern and with which we should therefore not be preoccupied (Marcus Aurelius, *Meditations*, IX, 6, *et passim*). There then remains the present alone in which your act is deployed and on which you can place your concentration. In the present moment, as fleeting as it is, we have everything: Is not the entire world implicated in the slightest event and its causal linkage? Since the quality of the moment cannot increase with duration and an instant of happiness is therefore equivalent to an eternity, one which can and must be discovered at once—we will never be happy other than in the immediate.... Not to put things off is the golden rule. But, having reached this point, the Stoic can now only repeat himself; he multiplies the imperatives for himself. It is no longer so much a matter of understanding as of convincing oneself: What in fact would there be to explain? On the other hand, the fact that one could not go (or would not need to go) further in the development of thought, is compensated by the work that needs to be done on the self, each day, each hour, so as not to allow living, which appears and falls short in its injunction, shamefully slip away.

Having no expectation of progress in the exposition, it will only be possible to progress through 'practice'—in the exercise (the 'spiritual exercises' on which Pierre Hadot[13] insists) of the *askesis*. In fact, in these precepts of wisdom, is it not a question of saturated (and satisfied) formulations which withdraw into themselves without disclosing a fissure, delivered as they are to memorization and to which therefore philosophy can add nothing and from which it expects nothing more? It is even on this precise point that they separate: philosophy develops in a history and always seeks to say more, in the pursuit of that fascinating stake of truth; 'wisdom', meanwhile, is 'without history'; saying as little as possible, it does not seek to attract attention and only individual sages have their own history—it would be impossible to compose a 'history of wisdom'. Likewise, we see ourselves condemned here to the truism by which we know philosophy can construct only by concealing it. This finally forces us to confront or, rather, drives us towards, this 'remember living', to that about which there is nothing to be said, to such an extent that it is true, *vrai*—so true that it is no longer interesting. This, conversely, reveals as a consequence that philosophy is not interested in *the whole* truth, as it claims, but, on the whole, with a very pellicular stratum of it—that which gives rise to contradiction and can contest itself, is enigmatic and therefore ties itself up in intrigue about which one can speculate.

Therefore, when it comes to 'living' (its importance), it will only be possible to operate its *variations*. This is not a possible question but a 'theme'; as the dance varies its figures, this theme belongs by right to poetry: 'Gather the day . . .'. Or, for the art of varying, we can trust Montaigne: 'I have a dictionary completely separate from me . . .'. The characteristic of metaphorical expression is to bring out what escapes not through its mystery but through its banality; Montaigne similarly made a continuous use of it. I once more 'fumble' for and 'hold' to the precious time of the present; I 'savour' and 'ruminate' on this 'sweetness' of living: this needs 'application' and strategy or, as Montaigne says, it takes 'housework' to enjoy it. Or his 'contentment', I do not 'skim' it but 'probe' it and 'bend' my reason in order to 'gather' it. . . .

That there is no need to go further in order to say it, and even that one must keep the discourse from forever going ahead (of being for ever dragged into its 'course'); that one should therefore work against the nature of its discursivity even so as to constrain it in the marking time which learns nothing more but rightly prevents a passing, as time 'passes', and holds back an advancing, this is what Montaigne intentionally puts to work in the tautology: 'When I dance, I dance' ('when I sleep, I sleep' . . .). In disappointing our expectation, in other words, in saying nothing more in the principal proposition than in the temporal which precedes and situates it, in other words still, by folding one onto the other and by completely reflecting the latter in the former, Montaigne indicates that the only thing that counts is being the contemporary of oneself, indeed, and putting up a barrier to the continual inclination to go beyond. What is the use of 'saying' it (that which is so true that it does not convince)? Can *expression* have a hold over this ineradicable propensity to outstrip? It would be better, on the uniform course of time, for a *moment* to be outlined or hollowed out, to bring squarely into play the 'dis'-'course', and against it, in that dispositive of the tautology, such a measure of retention.

What resource remains to make this immediacy of 'living' stand out, so that it neither remains without hold on the indistinctness of the transition, nor, on the contrary, is placed too conveniently at a distance under the transfigured spaces of 'true life', other than to introduce into it the *other* which differentiates it or, at least, to confront it with it? This means that, if one distrusts a separating into two, opening up an access point through some *negation* of it, which reopens the divergence, does it also spill over in *mediation* towards it? Already this is done by metaphor (in Montaigne), by 'transporting' it into the other. Or the most elementary, still totally external strategy—to bring living out from its sticking-point in the already-there and to be able to unsettle what is settled will be to make it arise from out of the opposition and to contrast it. Among the Stoics, in making the ungraspable present emerge from it through voluntaristic repression (to the point of denial?) at once of the future and the past—or in emphasizing the 'living' through rivalry with those who spoil it. Montaigne did something similar to Antiphon: I feel the sweetness of living along with others, but this is not, like them, 'in passing and slipping'. . . .

Or, again, what is the most ordinary procedure of wisdom—to 'enhance' living, like a flash, against the background of its contrary, death, *in umbra mortis*. Horace wrote: 'Convince yourself that each new day which rises will be your last'; for such is the consequence: 'then it is with gratitude that you will to able to find-your-place'; in other words, that in addition given, moreover, in gratification 'the hour will not be hoped for' (*Epistles*: 1.4.13–14; or 'We need to accomplish each action as if it was our last', and so on— Marcus Aurelius, *Meditations*: 2.5.2). Already, the same thing goes for sickness (Montaigne again): if health really is, according to the doctors' formula (Leriche[14]), 'life in the silence of the organs', bearing in consequence upon the ignorance of living within us, sickness, in taking its revenge, is what awakens this immediacy of living and makes it experience, even if through privation or suffering. The 'good use' of illnesses, in effect, but one which no longer prepares the way to edification and sanctity.

In this way living starts to be felt the day his eyes burst (we are imagining Oedipus at Colonus): he was no longer submerged by the immediate but the withdrawal of one capacity gave him access to the feelings of others, which he then discovered to be so generous. The sick person is able to rise and go to the window:

as if by an indentation, from below the tiredness, he receives, but infinitely, as a blow to his chest, the springtime of which he has been deprived. Sitting on the bench, like a sack, moving with difficulty, he suddenly feels with this heavy sack that it has become so miraculously open to those things he had until then too much of (vitality) to be able to apprehend. Seeking a sunnier spot, where he settles, he is amazed as he realizes the sweetness of what he had never yet experienced, even if it was so familiar and even if he had known so many springs and summers. He had until then not perceived the light, as it had risen on every day of his life—he started to see it only as he knew he was about to leave it.

Performances, in art, have constructed so many montages in order to organize this *access* (to the everyday of 'living' we do not perceive): it was necessary to undo one's clothes, pass under the hem of the swimming pool in order finally to discover, in re-emerging on the surface of the water, enclosed by high walls, a bit of sky (James Turrell in Poitiers[15])—the sky we each have every day before our eyes without seeing it, no matter how much attention we give to it, whose splendour we cannot even begin to imagine, as Lucretius said, but upon which humanity can still forever cast only an 'exhausted' look, *fessus satiate videndi* (*The Nature of Things*: 2.1038). An exhaustion which is not so much habit or lassitude—as psychology refers our two facilities to it when this is not morality—than an incapacity to raise ourselves to what is simply 'given', *es gibt*. Such an operation, that one or another, essentially aims at this—to arrange a minimum of mediation (negation) to cross (to have to overcome in order to obtain) in such a way as finally to be able to capture this 'here' and 'now' of living which by its immediacy eludes us.

3

I nevertheless hear this amazement: Is it not possible simply (*immediately*) to apprehend this 'here' and 'now'? And is this not even precisely what 'living' is? Is it not the first mode of certainty? 'Living' would be deployed in this immediate knowing of the immediacy which gives us trust in a world (the very one Jacobi called by that extremely dubious term, *belief*). Therefore it is also for us to know how to consider it in an immediate way, when we examine it, welcoming it as it is presented, without altering it in any way or projecting onto it a preliminary conception or condition, without interfering with it and disturbing it. It is only here, now, that I 'live', says each 'self' opening its eyes (each time) at the heart of that presence and that contact.

Here-now, before that tree and under this ray of light, in that place and this hour: by plunging myself into the shimmering and rustling of these countless leaves, as by still more attentively following the slightest indentation or veining sketched of each of them—and even how would we get to the end of this plenitude so generously settled? It is deployed without limits, in space as in time, and one can also endlessly sink into its slightest detail: Is not the knowledge I take from it immediately announced as inexhaustible in its rush of impressions? At the same time as it appears the most 'true', since I have taken nothing from its object, have not interfered with it through the work of my mind and not yet begun to construct it. My thought has not yet been set in motion to invest it and break it up, not yet conceived of it as a system of relations, not yet distributed it according to a multitude of characters or properties. I keep it in front of me, intact in its dispensed profusion, immerged as I myself am in what is concrete, and nothing yet intervenes to separate me from it. What need would I therefore have to 'gain access' to this perceptible paradise, since it is already given to me? Unless only lost paradises exist. . . .

Hegel had the skill to show how this first and immaculate relation, at whose bosom I believe I have been unquestionably fulfilled, that I would like to preserve over everything since it is within it that I feel myself living, is already always cracked (see the first pages of *Phenomenology*)—and this occurs with itself and is inevitable. Hegel had the skill to reveal how there is a snare in this initial access, so firmly do we think we are able to adhere to it; consequently, what naivety we reveal when we 'believe' we live in an immediate opening onto the world, and entrust ourselves to what is perceptible (this is his response to Jacobi). Does not the certainty which overpowers me when facing this tree, at a particular moment of the day, under that ray of light, ineluctably have to give way to an other, at the very heart of my apprehension? I think *here* but, as soon as I move my head, this *here* ceases to exist; I think *now*, but this has immediately passed—the process of negation, as Hegel noted, has always *already* begun. I have in mind that tree, as unique as it is, but barely have I said 'tree' to myself than its singularity is immediately lost—the mediation of language causes me to tip over into generality. From this concrete example, this pure 'self' (which I am and which has not yet developed into consciousness) withholds nothing. What I 'aim' at in my mind is 'stale' (*schal*, as Hegel says) and emptied. Or what I retain of it is its contrary—a 'here' of all 'heres', abstracted from each of them; or a 'now' that one can pronounce indifferently at any moment. This 'tree-here' equally expresses all the others that I see. Barely have I spoken of the immediacy in which to live than it flees; barely have I wanted to grasp this plenitude than it becomes wretchedly impoverished.

It will readily be conceded that neither this here nor that now towards which I aim, nor this self that I am when confronted with them, remain—they each carry on dissociating themselves from themselves. On one side as on the other, as soon as I name them, even if only to myself, I see them capsize into abstraction. Would not the immediacy of living be contained in their relation rather than within them? But can I hold myself in the immediacy of the relation which links one to the other, the relation which is alone reliable and is what constitutes my certitude, in spite of the reversal which each of these terms entailed? If I keep to the unity of this very relation, as universal as it is, then immediacy is found within it. Let us not therefore allow ourselves to be distracted from this impression that I see and attach ourselves to it in an enduring and heroic way (which is Cartesian but takes on inverse resolutions). I will stay looking at this tree without imagining that I could look elsewhere, or that I could distribute it in a multiplicity of heres. Neither will I compare this here or now to some other will keep from dreaming of an other self able to see something else still. In short, I will remain plunged in this 'pure intuition' (*reines Anschauen*).

As profoundly as I then let myself be occupied, a demarcation always stands out, philosophy states in the face of this naive certitude—difference has always already been engaged. Even if this would first be between 'me' on the one hand and 'the thing' on the other: I have certainty only through the thing and the thing exists in certitude only through me; consequently the one is such, Hegel concludes, only as *mediated* by the other (*vermittelt*). In other words, all of a sudden and all in one go, the mediation silently infiltrates the assurance I believed to be most immediate and starts moving towards its surpassing.

In this Hegel is convincing: all of the initial immediacy which has been presented is *cracked*—it is already undermined by scission, threatened by a longer work of mediation. The immediacy in which living, since it is not acquired at the beginning, will only be the of the order of a result; it arises not from a given but from an effect. Likewise, Hegel grounded himself in such a way as to designate the discrepancy which becomes marked out between what is aimed at and the spoken word (*meinen* and *sprechen*): I 'aim' is the most singular and concrete but, as soon as I speak about it, I express the opposite, namely, what is poorest and most general. For all that, what can be drawn from it? Is this necessarily the conclusion which Hegel came to or, rather, did he already have it under his belt? Since it is not there at the beginning, this work of mediation, located from the outset between the self and the world and which language deploys, has to take that very long road (the only one there is) by which consciousness is conquered, passing through negation and suffering, leading to completion and teleologically to the adequacy in which one is reconciled in the other (in 'absolute nowing')?

Admittedly, we recognize this immediacy in which living is the order, not of the initial, but of a process, contrary to common belief; it is necessary to *accede* to it. But is it for all that of the order of the End? Can we conceive of any other progress than according to this Way of the Cross developing in stages, in doubt and despair, as Hegel continues it, until the lost immediate, which has been so long postponed, is revealed as the conclusion of History—the expected Salvation? Above all: Can other strategies of access to the immediate not be conceived through the word? Hyppolite, in his commentary, poses the question in a note which undermines the edifice at one go: 'One of the profound vices of Hegelianism is perhaps revealed here in this philosophy of language and in this conception of the singularity . . .'. But why, good god, leave it in a footnote?

Hegel, in other words, grounded himself so as to give full rights to the word, no matter what rupture or breakage it entails, at the risk that we would otherwise be enclosing ourselves in an ineffable which allows the sensible to sink into confusion and the self into unconsciousness. But is getting the mediation of the word to intervene the only way to embark on that odyssey of *logos* in which all the figures of truth are threaded one after the other, all of them disappointing but all integrated, and to the point of apotheosis— that of a Universal which needs to pass through so many particular contradictions in order *to become* Singular (needed to cross such a range of time for the Now of identity to occur)? In passing through the word, do we for all that trust in its *discursivity*, of which the dialectic marks the apogee? Can we not conceive of a mediation of the word proceeding inversely, by which I mean not allowing itself to be dragged along by this discursivity but thwarting and interrupting it, thereby short-circuiting the mediation engaged in rather than deploying it? It will cause the immediate to surge forth not *after* (*in fine*) but at the very heart of the mediation, or of its *between*, even if this causes it to implode.

4

Poetry has been this other way of mobilizing the word, contradicting mediation at the same time as it puts it to work—the word as *mediate-immediate*, and not handed over to the very long detour of mediation that alone arrests its conclusion. Poetry *realizes* a here and now, since they are not given initially, but this is not staked on a future, as in Hegel, with the completion of the *logos* and the end of philosophy: such is the poetic 'effect' (it is also the order of the result) but which does not have the patience of the concept and has no expectation. The poem does not even need to be finished in order to succeed—each verse is contemporary with itself and bears its plenitude within it (which is how I would define a verse). This will be perceived better still from outside a Western culture that is so marked with the *logos* and where poetry has so often been nothing more than a rhymed discourse. From early on, having been in contrast distrustful of discursive linkage, the traditions of the Far East have especially enhanced strategies which could thwart it, slanting, breaking or inhibiting it; and as it constitutes part of the common activity while inhabiting the everyday, in them poetry has been considered a means of privileged access to the immediate in which to live. 'Has been': Perhaps it is necessary from now on to put it in the past?

In order to cut short the discursive temptation, so as to create ingress into the immediate, but without delay or postponement, the most elementary thing is to be satisfied with the brief form. This maintains the word in its springing up, withheld from becoming *settled* or from 'spreading out'. The quatrain from the Tang era exploits its possibility to the limit:

> *Light boat welcome high guest*
> *From a far lake above to come*
> *Before balustrade facing cup (of) wine*
> *(The) four sides of the lotus open*

(Wang Wei n.d.: 245).

There is not so much an economy of means here, as has so often been said, as an elliptical and decanted arrangement of an *access*—the word succeeds in expressing, by being married with its movement, the dawning of a *moment*. From two courses which, departing from two sides, from two shorelines, converge and encounter each other and result in a 'before', an 'in relation' (*dui*)—facing the lake, facing the guest (*v*3). But, hardly has the here and now appeared, between the welcoming and welcomed, than it immediately leads, at one fell swoop, onto a complete and integral seizure, to which nothing can be added, that no divergence or lack will contrast or fissure, since plenitude no longer finds anything threatening in it: 'from all sides'—'the lotus'—'open'. Any thought of another 'here' or another 'now', tipping the 'here' and 'now' into abstraction, is thereby (*ipso facto*) dissipated. There is really progression and access at the same time as there is self-realization of presence in reaching immanence—the immediate emerges as do the flowers at the water's level. The absolute is not attained after a long detour, as is the case in Hegel, but through a cutting short. But this is of course without involving any sort of division between the 'self'/'world', of a mediation of one through the other and a comparison.

How to 'aim' at a moment whose sufficiency as an instant is such that there is no need for us to think about some other time, or which is so complete as landscape that we are given no pause to dream of an elsewhere, which is unconcerned about a here which would no longer be here or by a now which would already have passed? Not because such a moment would be exceptional but, precisely, because it is ordinary—in it the here and now are gathered into an impression whose affirmed ephemeral quality has banished the ephemeral; the place which is hollowed out dispenses with all localization. This here can contain as much *here* as you like, as this now is *all* possible nows, not because it conceals or subsumes them but, we might say, because they absorb them:

> *Autumn mountain gathering rest clarity*
> *Flight bird follows before companion*
> *Colour azure moment separate clear*
> *Evening clouds not to have place (where) to rest*

(ibid.: 244).

This moment is nevertheless really that of every passage: an autumn—an evening—a flight of birds—contrasting plays of shadow and light—clouds evolving restlessly. But the tensions they organize weave a net from it into which so many moments and landscapes allow themselves to fall. The pursuit is opposed to the gathering (as springing up is to extinction, $v1$–2) just as distinction responds to veiling (and place to time, $v3$–4)—because the moment-world is complete in its various interactions, it therefore calls upon no postponement. Nothing in it is symbolic, but no concrete offers an obstruction to it; nothing is named in it as a self-subject, but for all that the scene does not tip into the descriptive. Thwarting the opposition between saying and not saying, from saying which never ends just as much as the enclosing in the unspeakable, the poem barely speaks but does so in a total way. Nothing is lacking in it. Could anything be added to it? What dialectic of the universal and the particular could still intervene? Some singular is grasped, on this threshold raised by language, as available for any apprehension.

As in this exchange of quatrains between Wang Wei and Pei Di, the *hokku* of Japanese poetry, an initial verset then cited in isolation (later commonly called haiku), 'fixes' some here and now in their *springing up*. It responds as tit for tat (to the friend or the landscape), grasps it in flight, grasps it as *such*: this reactivity no longer leaves a fissure, by its sudden mobilization, between 'aiming' and 'saying' (*meinen* and *sagen*)— between what passes through the mind and what one expresses. The risk of seeing the word led astray by abstraction is blocked by this idiosyncrasy constituting itself in the *moment*. 'Flowers which fly in the wind, leaves which fall—if we don't fix them in open movement, by sight or hearing, their scattering—once reduced to immobility, their very life will have vanished without leaving a trace' (Bashō). Or, again, 'The light which emanates from things has to be fixed in words before it might become extinguished in the mind'. The immediacy of living then shoots up from the contrast between the 'invariant' and the 'flowing' (*fuéki-ryûkô*). In relation to this, all evocation, as fugitive and local as it would be, forms a whole:

From Karasaki
The pine more than the flowers
Veiled by mist.

It is whole and sufficient. The poem is closed, to the extent that it awaits nothing more, lacks nothing. Once again: What could be added to it? There really is attainment and *access* there—what is intuited does not claim to be an initial given; but this mediation by the word is accomplished in immediacy and suddenness. In fact, that some here and now would thereby be grasped, 'fixed' by improvisation and trapped in emotion, is rendered possible only by the process of maturation which leads to it and, in its effect, alone allows this *fresh* approach to the world ('fresh' as I have said 'innocent')—we finally look at things, in front of us, as if for the first time. On the one hand, this means that, for the poet (but each person is potentially a poet), *to train* is a matter for the whole of life, one must work without respite in order to raise the receptive-perceptive quality of one's mind; on the other hand, an impression must be translated into the verset 'from the same movement': 'Do not allow a hair's breath between the writing tablet and yourself'. Then 'when the hour comes for arranging the tablet, consider it as worthless scrawl'—do not attach yourself to what is no longer a living word but always remain ready to find a path for yourself in language (Bashō: §3–7). In this way, if we know how to be ceaselessly 'lying in wait for things', ready to gather them, Bashō says once more, the impressions they arouse 'will of themselves come in versets'; while, if such preparation for capturing the springing up is lacking, we are reduced to 'making a poem'—in other words, the effort will be vain, it will be that of 'dextrous' folk who remain prisoners of their own viewpoints and do not know how to give a welcome. Training and vigilance are needed to allow nothing to coagulate (to get bogged down) in the here and now—let us not sterilize our sensations, even if this means only remaining too long in the same place, near the same people, in immobilizing relations. During the last years of his life Bashō endlessly changed his home.

5

Far from giving access to it, linking it, continuity and discursivity (causality) are obstacles to grasping the here and now. As soon as we liberate *zen* (*chan* in Chinese) from the irrationalism and fantasies through which the West delights in concealing it, rigorously (and logically) it does not express anything else—it is the continuous threading of our thoughts which, by being woven through abstraction, obfuscates the immediacy of living. If I start speaking, says the master to his disciples, I will do so without stopping again, during *kalpas*[16] as innumerable as the grains of sand in the Ganges, I will be there trying to 'pin' you down and to pin you again by my words, and this delay will not end: How can we emerge from the 'transmigration' (*samsara*) which is simply another name for this everlasting Postponement? It is useless either to confide in the spoken word and to embark upon an interminable mediation, or to enclose oneself comfortably in a silence that prevents all access, which the word alone can release ('under the word': *yan xia*). While all discourse is drawn towards still further repression, and to fix itself in a precept just as to codify itself in truth, one will need, consequently, to promote an anti-discursive use of the word and in such a way as to protect oneself from *settling* it.

It will need to be said, but 'said quickly'. 'Make me a sentence', but one which will be decisive—which no longer links up the thoughts of before and after but finally breaks the thread of ideas instead of following them and bursts out immediately without our hesitating (as soon as you hesitate, the Master beats you), no longer allowing the speaker and the listener to be distinguished from each other ('welcoming' and 'welcomed'; which is one and which is the other?) and might lead us to cease even wondering whether or not we have understood. A sentence which is no longer 'thought' but is reactive, which does not express but leaves half-open, no longer knowing either degree or 'stepping-stone', having the same shock effect in the course of the exchange, between the interlocutors placed under tension, as a *khât*, a belch, a *cha*, a slap or being hit with a stick; developing nothing notional, it suddenly lets it go by. This occurs immediately and not after—it 'awakens' or gives access, crossing through all the obstructions accumulated by the mediations at one fell swoop through a breaking open.

In order to stem this endless sequence, from which suffering, that of discourse as of existences, inexhaustibly renews itself, it will be necessary not to be afraid of placing the word in contradiction with itself. It will be necessary not to dread systematically cutting away all of its possibilities—of affirmation as well as of negation, as of affirmation and negation at once; of undoing the alternatives and the ties, of not adopting one part or the other. If it is appropriate to reveal the void inherent in the world, it will still not satisfy this Vacuity (and inevitably reconstitute it as an entity); if it is appropriate to denounce Mâra, trust should equally not be placed in Buddha: 'Mâra and

Buddha are both to be beaten' (Linji Yixuan).[17] Up to the point that, such is the access, when no longer holding to one or the other, we suddenly realize the fundamental equivalence of these opposites (what is called *coming out of duality*). The Awakening is nothing other than realizing (in an immediate way) this equivalence.

It must still be understood that this 'realization' is opposed to knowledge (this is why the sudden taking hold of the *zen* is not the evidence of classical philosophy); and to do so is to understand it in the two senses of the term: to realize is to make it happen in a effective way (to realize the Buddha in oneself: to make it happen); but to also take account and become aware (that it is already real, already such, in the English sense of *to realize*, which classical Chinese already expressed in relation to moral consciousness: *si* in *Mencius*). Thereby we may know that a relative is dead, but we do not always manage to 'realize' it. In the same way, the 'nature of the Buddha' has always been within me; it is merely necessary for me to 'grasp' it here and now, so that this 'thereby' exists (*tatha, zhenru*). But this *thereby*, precisely because it is immediate, is what is most difficult of access (it requires finding a gap in the continuous veil of mediations); and this is why strategies that appear so disconcerting are needed.

If I want to come to the aid of the 'here' and the 'now', Hegel says by way of a concession, not to let myself be taken into the trap of divergence which inevitably opens up between 'aiming' and 'expressing', can I not be content with pointing my finger and showing (*auf-zeigen*)? I will designate this *here* with a gesture (but the here shown immediately decomposes no less, anew, into a multitude of heres: one in front and one behind, a high / a low, a left / a right and so on; and, in the same way, the now which my watch points to decomposes into an infinity of nows (hours, minutes, seconds and so on). I can never do more than even indicate some here or now that might be. But pointing with a finger has become the most familiar *zen* action because it is the most pedagogical. Whenever he was asked a question, Master Ju Zhi[18] ('Finger which indicates') always responded by silently raising a finger (but he sliced off the finger of anyone who imitated him: let us not leave anything fixed in a rut)—he was content to point out the immediacy of the *thereby*, of any *thereby*.

In order to respond to the customary questions examining the absolute (according to these conventional terms: 'What is the Buddha?' 'Why did Bodhidharma come from the south of India to China?' and so on), the *zen* Master designates the first thing which comes into his head: the 'cypress in the courtyard'

(Zhao Zhou); or 'three pounds of linen' (Dong Shan: he was weighing linen). As soon as one has understood, or better 'realized', that only the immediate exists (the Buddha present in himself), whose endless mediations of language entice us away, everything which comes to hand, in other words, anything which gushes forth from the immediate, can refer to this immediacy and express the absolute. From that point, when the fundamental equivalence of things has been grasped, anything, in an equivalent way, can point out this equivalence.

It is certainly not in the name of some sort of realism that *zen* grasps the absolute in the immediacy of the *this*. Even more than Hegel, the *zen* Master is aware that the 'tree' 'I' perceive at the moment is different from the 'same' tree 'I' perceived just a moment before; and the same thing goes for the eye which is perceiving it (and for the 'this-me' which looks at it): both are merely the products of the discriminating function of the mind which extracts and stabilizes them as entities (in hypostasis) by bringing into play language's function of articulation. Likewise, the only way of thwarting it, of making the 'thereby', to which all of this teaching is reduced, spring up, in other words, in order to produce *access*, is to open a breach in the heart of that illusion by cutting its mediation short. This is why the *zen* Master appeals to re-activity, for which everything serves, whether the insult, the *khât* or striking with a stick. As soon as the spontaneity is recovered from underneath the causalist sequence, there is no longer even any need to 'aim': everything can be invested in its plenitude, including the most everyday actions, behaving in the most ordinary way (to be 'without business' [Linji])—and finding oneself at every turn in the 'way' (*tao*). As soon as there is nothing further to create an obstruction to the *springing* up of the thereby, the slightest circumstantial statement which comes to mind can *equally* be the essential response. As in *haiku*, it delivers at one fell swoop the whole of 'living'.

6

One day when he was asked how to go beyond the dilemma of the word and silence, from the silence which inhibited the manifestation and the word which alters it, a *zen* Master did so by responding: 'I will always remember the springtime landscape I saw one day in the Jiangnan region. The partridges were then clucking among the flowers in all their brilliance.' To open a breach which finally reveals, giving at one fell swoop the answer to every question envisaged or even not considered, the Master here adopts an inverse strategy to the ones considered earlier—he does not invoke immediacy by breaking with the interminable mediations of language (through a decisive sentence or by striking with a stick) but by evoking a past impression which serves as a mediation for the capacity of Realization, here and now, in other words, what we call *Awakening*. We have such difficulty in accessing our immediate impressions due to the very fact of their immediacy—it leaves us without a hold over them. This is why they remain diffuse, inconsistent, disappointing and evanescent; hence, we accuse them of unreality, although they alone bear in their hollows the 'thereby' of things. But here is, through the unexpected and anecdotal reappearance of one past impression, the perception of an effective here and now, through an effect of perspective or ricochet, suddenly lightening up, collecting together and totalizing itself. As distanced as it might be in space as in time, the past impression suddenly draws a plenitude in which to live from the fact of being buried—the clucking of the partridge and scent of the flowers. Its backward movement brings a jolt; thanks to the divergence, due to absence, everything is rendered all at once to presence. The present impression does not lift itself up to it, dispersed as it is in a flux that is continuous and impossible to define. There is a resurgence in it, a reminiscence, which through its eruption opens up access but not for all that to memory. Everything in Proust is also contained here.

Just as when he makes the discovery of it at the end of the work when, in the library of the prince of Guermantes on that last morning, the Narrator waits for the completion of the piece of music he is performing, for Proust too it is a matter of *access*, in a decisive and total sense: 'One has knocked at all the doors which lead nowhere' for so many years 'and then one stumbles without knowing it on the only door through which one can enter—which one might have sought in vain for a hundred years, and it opens of its own accord' (1992b). This access, in which every search ends, is really, for the Narrator, an access to 'living', and even to the 'sole milieu where he can live', that suddenly reveals the past impression arising in the sensation of the here and now: 'So great was my appetite for living now that, three times, a veritable moment of the past had been reborn in me' (ibid.).

Whether it is a question of such a moment or any other, as the Narrator sees them from then on in a cascade, from the shock of the unequal paving stones in Piazza San Marco, in Venice, a reappearance of the paving stones of the courtyard of a Parisian hotel, or from the open window over the sea in Balbec, reappearing in the starched stiffness of the serviette on

which the Narrator wipes his mouth before entering
the salon (or the shock of a hammer heard against the
wheel of a train in a station deep in the woods one
early morning, and brought back to life in the sound
of a teaspoon against a plate while the buffet was
being prepared)—this sudden and unexpected resurgence cuts short the endless intellectual deliberations,
interrupts the sterile linkage and contingency. It gives
rise to an 'awakening' which, here equally, once it is
produced, is definitive and gives rise to the *thereby*. A
plenitude finally becomes accessible which, in this
case as well, suddenly instigates a remarkable joy which
covers up everything and liberates all at once. This discovery results not from one more argument or some
more convincing reason, but here we find that, under
the effect of such a revelation, all the difficulties which
have been presenting a stumbling block suddenly fade
away, 'lifted as if by an enchantment'.

Proust illuminates why this sudden resurgence of
a past impression into the present sensation furnishes
the open sesame of the desired access, and, because of
this, decomposes it. There is in this a simultaneity of
presence and absence, a mediation by means of the
reminiscence which causes an immediacy of the sensation to stand out. Instead of what we see throughout the day—whereas the latter, the present sensation,

continues like a haemorrhage to flow out and might never be able to be 'collected', as the adage nevertheless had it, hoping to stop it in its passage. Because in one case, as in the other, we 'languish': as much in the observation of the present where the senses, saturated with the immediate, allow nothing essential to be discerned as in the consideration of the past which the intelligence 'dries up' by calling it to mind in a forced way. But, in the case of the involuntary resurgence at the heart of the present sensation of a past impression, the *distance* which alone can create an emphasis (and so play the imagination which alone 'delights beauty', says Proust, attached to the traditional theory of the faculties) and the *actuality* of sensory perception which alone can confer effectivity to an existence are combined at once. In Proustian terms, there is in this at once a 'disturbance' of the senses mobilized by the present and an 'idealization' of the impression through decantation and promotion thanks to the past. Only the superimposition of the two, remembrance and sensation, can under this double pressure produce the exceptional emergence of a *moment* that saves itself from the continuous and irksome flux of 'time' and is suddenly free to unfurl its inexhaustible plenitude. For there to be *access* to it, it is in fact necessary for there to be at once a crossing (to cross the temporal depth leading to success) and the possibility of encountering or, above all, of immediately operating—and in a plain way—whatever unexpectedly disengages the present sensation.

The whole problem of Proust, once what this phenomenon of involuntary memory presents as a resource that is exceptional and forming salvation is revealed (the *petite madeleine*), is really to convert it into strategy—to transform what at the beginning is only a 'marvellous expedient of nature', painting in glowing colours the sensation at once in the past and in the present, into a viable and durable way for achievement. No longer to remain in this *trompe l'oeil* causing a fugitive coincidence of the two sensations and which on the whole, as Proust recognizes, is only a 'subterfuge'. In a different way to voluntary memory, what validates this sudden resurgence in terms of truth is precisely its unexpected character; that it escapes my initiative, in other words, is not produced by the interference of my mind. But how then to make something of it other than a piece of luck or, rather, a miracle?

Starting from that point, how are we to demand a mastery and choice of means when the old Stoic moral precept, of grasping the fleeting present through an effort of one's attentiveness, has once more been replayed? We know even before we begin that it will be disappointing to return to those places, whether Balbec or Venice, from which such a profusion of impressions suddenly emerged. These places did not deliver up such a plenitude when one was on the spot, when the distance which alone made them emerge could be put into play: separation, the condition of mediation which alone allows accession, was lacking. As for recalling to mind these places today, at his table—to describe them, with closed eyes, is to reconstitute a sequence which is inevitably abstract and no longer retains anything living in its net.

Without there being a will to aestheticization, the result can only be aesthetic and ethical at the same time, mingling art and living in an inseparable way (and so giving meaning back to the old, finally retrievable, formula of the 'art of living'). But that literature might be the only solution, which it erects as a vocation, is the result not so much of it leading, as Proust said, from 'impression' to 'expression'; still less of the fact that it could carve out and perpetuate sensation. No, the characteristic of literature and what makes of it a decisive matter, bearing revelation, is not there at all. What forms its destination is that it generalizes (systematizes), and especially legitimates, the path that gives access to the immediate (to the absolute) through mediation. It is in this that it is strategic and effectively furnishes means or engagements. The whole of *Recherche du temps perdu* turns, in fact, upon this unique truth, delivered *in fine*, and whose resurgence from past impression into present sensation was nothing but the heralding indication— we 'become aware of' 'the beauty of one thing' only 'in another' (1992b). This is to admit that in itself sensation is obtuse: it is always in the process of dissipating, delivering almost nothing of itself, or in such a superficial way, because there is nothing in it which allows for recognition and inspection of it—because we cannot take sufficient distance to grapple with it. It cannot be gathered up and defined—it cannot be placed in a 'vase', as Proust said, and its immediacy is sterile. On the other hand, when it is transported into an other (a 'metaphor' in the proper sense), with the mediation once again intervening in its respect, its quality finally appears.

If the access to living, such as literature reveals it, is therefore in the *mediation* of a thing by (through) the other, that one can erect it in principle and even as a unique principle, in the fact that one fundamentally reveals oneself only in the other, or that an impression is effectively delivered up only by means of an equivalence, because if it is reduced simply to the immediate present, it cannot be gathered, and there is then no further need for a Platonic *division into two*, between appearance and Being, instigating the same as a truth, founding what is transient as identity—the *metaphor*, as a transfer of one into the other, is sufficient to bring out its 'beauty'. It organizes the precise relation of presence and absence, of an elsewhere giving rise to presence which fulfils our aspirations. From that point there is no further need to project another world, another level, another life— 'true life': the world is fully illuminated through the play of these internal mediations. The metaphor, in other words, has replaced the metaphysical—all that is needed is literature defined as a work of putting in relation, expressing one by the other, of which Proust fixes the regulating principle, even if such a relation, he recognized, might in itself 'not be very interesting' and its objects 'mediocre'. No doubt it is to this very virtue of transposition, so much more than to its emphasis of the singular, as is ordinarily said, that literature owes to its having become the postmetaphysical discourse of modernity.

Nonetheless, because he did not hold this principle throughout, Proust at times returned in spite of himself to a metaphysical setting—through convenience of representation of course (by which language

is so well broken in) even more than due to the so-
often-invoked influence of the spiritualism of his age.
But we no longer read these idealist formulae except
as dross: the Narrator wants to enjoy the 'essence of
things' in their 'permanence', by 'escaping' the present,
he seeks 'celestial nourishment' in an 'extra-temporal'
being, and so on. This distorts the function of the
metaphor itself: 'by comparing a quality common to
two sensations', the writer will '(extract) their common
essence and (reunite) them to each other, liberated
from the contingencies of time, within a metaphor'
(ibid.). Would the metaphor thereby proceed from the
concerted act of a 'reuniting'? Would it not, rather, take
advantage of its unexpectedness (in which it remains
of the immediate in its mediation)? In addition, the
Narrator, forgetful of 'living', from that moment logically comes to oppose 'true life' to life, which: 'though
it ought to be more precious to us than anything in
the world, yet remains ordinarily for ever unknown to
us, the discovery of our true life' (Proust 1992a) From
which a discreet tipping over follows in which literature inevitably assumes the value of a substitution:
true 'life . . . is literature' (ibid.).

Why would this 'common' that has become evident between a past impression and the present sensation 'extract', as Proust wanted, the ordinary path

from the metaphysical which inevitably leads him to want to abstract an 'essence' from it? Does not this sudden 'hesitation' to which the Narrator is carried, in extreme cases no longer knowing where he is, even if only for a brief moment, in Venice or Paris, on Piazza San Marco, or in the hotel courtyard, and 'stumbling' and indecisive, between 'past and present places', once again arise from a phenomenon of *ambiguity*, in other words, from equivalence and the demarcation becoming impossible, in which 'living' is plunged, no longer allowing definition, at the same time as he works, starting from the holdings (*fonds*) from which it seeps out, to emphasize the differences? This occurs therefore without there being any need to assume some substance or substratum 'exempt from the order of time' and, consequently, from reinscribing this phenomenological into ontology. For the problem of access (to the here and now) is that of our *per*-ceptive capacity, without it being necessary for all that to break through a curtain of perceptible illusions and to denounce appearances. It is strategic without implying conversion to another order of reality. The here and now not being directly graspable, it is necessary to approach them indirectly.

The metaphor differs at once from both one and the other—from the comparison which is a mediate mediation, pegged by its 'like', and has been patiently worked ever since Homer extended it at length and, in the same way but from the other side, what Proust calls the *cinematographic parade of things*, by staying with simple data and suppressing the possibility of relation and mediation, which is thereby immediately thought to be realistic but is actually sterile. For in its functioning, the metaphor is an immediate mediation, and it is in this way that it is exemplary—in its suddenness, it brings to the surface the very thing it transports into the other; it immediately gives access at the same time as it allows a crossing. In this way it effects a *trans*-appearance.

7

The problem that is posed, or the concept henceforth required, is effectively more that of *transparency* than of 'appearance'. It is less to denounce appearance or plead for it, according to the old debate philosophy has developed throughout its history (Plato against the Sophists or, inversely, Nietzsche in revolt against classical idealism), than to comprehend that there is no effective appearance except if it *trans*-appears. In other words, there is no immediately given initial appearance, or not one that can be discerned—there is no more initial appearance than a first beginning—

it is not the first time that the curtain has been raised on the world and reveals it. But there appears only that which, in *crossing* the other, finds itself to be revealed in it. Having perceived metaphorical logic according to which an impression is suddenly delivered up in its plenitude only when transported into another, it was logical for Proust to describe the new material in which to compose his work by its 'transparency'. As in Mallarmé: Will it be possible to grasp the 'virgin, perennial and beautiful today', other than through the 'transparent glacier of flights unflown'? But is there not a temptation in this to return, once more, to Platonism, for 'not having sung the land where living . . .'.

The *Zhuangzi* evokes such transparency precisely in relation to 'living', and it does so at the conclusion of a strategy of hygiene which is one of a gradual disengagement beyond all the links which create opacity and form an obstruction (Chapter VI, 'Da zong shi'). This is called *the transparency of the morning*: an old woman is questioned about the way which has allowed her to stay so fresh, retaining the complexion of a young girl in spite of her great age. Giving an account of how she has progressed in stages, she presents it as a disencumbering which finally reveals. In her capacity to gather and keep her vitality within herself, she details how she found herself in a position, after three days, to treat the world as 'external', that is, to disoccupy herself from it; then, after seven days, to treat all things, all beings, as external; then, after nine days, to treat life itself as external. There was then nothing to shackle her capacity for living, not even concern about her life. This enabled her to gain access, she said, to the 'transparency of the morning', following which she was finally in a position to 'see' (*jian du*). As the commentator (Guo Xiang) makes it clear: 'As soon as we cease to be concerned about life, we cease to be afraid of death; no longer fearing death, we at once gain access in peace to everything we take on: in a way that is suddenly a clearing, there is no further obstruction (*huoran wu zhi*); in this we find a spontaneous spirit and we rises and act. This is what is called *the transparency of the morning* (*zhao che*): "morning-passing through"' (see the accompanying expression in the chapter 'Tiandi' in Guo 1983: *jian xiao yan*, p. 441).

Brought back to 'living', transparency is the result where the capacity of living suddenly becomes acuteness because it no longer allows itself to be bogged down by anything—not by the world, not by things, not by life. But why is this transparency associated with 'the morning'? Lovers of the light know why—

in the morning, the curtain of mist which the heat of the day accumulates has not yet extended, there is as yet no obfuscation from the dust rising from activity. The morning is the moment of transparency in which the light is in its freshness and entirely passes through—it illuminates and makes forms stand out obliquely, without overwhelming them. But it is especially because the world appears, in the morning, to have *passed through the night*. We would apprehend nothing of the morning if it did not spring forth from the veiling of darkness—we might see it but we would not perceive it. For the morning is no more a first beginning than there is a beginning of the world but it experiences itself as a beginning through the mediation it has with the night. If we did not need to gain access to this immediacy of the day, the day would not be noticed. Or, if we did not have eyelids but always had to keep our eyes open, we should perceive nothing. But, in rising from the night, the morning engages a capacity of beginning which a pure beginning could never have, and indeed it reopens possibilities. The same thing is true for ourselves, as Mencius notes (VI.a.8): our nature, in the morning, on awakening, reacts in an open way by straightaway following its positive inclination, without particular interests intervening yet in a way which give rise to the business of the day and progressively obscures and hide it from us.

Yesterday evening, the page could not be completed and one's thoughts vainly went round in circles—no path appeared any more certain than any other and no advance seemed possible. Had I been deluding myself? I fumble and do not see how I can possibly emerge from it. Then the next morning, when I awaken, everything suddenly becomes distinctly clear in my mind and has resolved itself; everything is ordered and stands out with clarity—there is a transparency and distinctness of ideas. One would them like to write straightaway, seize upon it immediately without having to speak to anyone else, to move, knowing that this clarity which has sprung up will soon dissipate. Rousseau loved to dictate from his bed to the 'lady of the house' when she came in the early morning to relight his fire. For it is not only the fact that, having rested, the material has decanted, or that the mind has continued to work silently during sleep, without our having dreamed about it, benefiting from this deferment, or that the sleep has allowed the resources of the intelligence to be reconstituted. But also the morning coincides with the emergence, giving back a possibility of *springing up*, of 'rising', before the day has started to spread out.

The world appears from the fact that it *trans-*appears from the night. From what night? From all nights. In one of Bergman's films which, as each time, plunges into laceration and culpability, excavates passionately the suffering and the absurd, the final scene is the rising of a new day: in the early morning, the itinerant and carefree actors go as a family along the river bank, in their trailer, the children playing cheerfully on the beach with all of the shadows having dissipated. This freshness and innocence is understood only to the extent that one needed to go through torment to end up in the here and now of a new day as it begins, rising as though it was the first day, something as simple as 'falling off a log', banal and miraculous, as every day is. Fabulous (and vertiginous) in spite of its ordinariness (or because of it) but that ordinarily one no longer sees or, rather, has never seen. One never sees what is always seen. According to an old *zen* aphorism, but which could equally well be a watchword of surrealism: the miracle of man is not to walk in the sky or on the water, but to walk on the ground. But how to 'realize' this miracle (of the ordinary), that is, to give an account of it, without still projecting onto it some causalism (interventionism), and doing so in a way which would in fact be (strictly) realist? By purging it of the religious as by washing out lyricism? The immediate, just like the simple, the natural and the ordinary, does not perceive itself; it is possible to gain access to it only as we gain access to the immediacy of the day from the night. Or, as it is necessary to have crossed Sodom and Gomorrah[19] in order one morning to have finally reached the capacity to catch the infinity of an impression, so forming a revelation, by unexpectedly banging one's foot against a paving stone.

In fact, the error is equally one and the other: to believe naively that a world in which living can initially be given to us, in its immediacy—paradise has already been definitively lost; or to commit oneself to attaining it in a mediation which never ends, the discourse-reason one then puts to work, *logos*, postponing still further the possibility of grappling with it. A world in which living 'is' not right away (in which respect metaphysics is correct), it is necessary to cause it to *rise*, but without again being concealed by whatever has been entrusted with revealing it; without what should be opening a path towards it no longer being able, in its never-ending course, to bring us back to it. This world or the 'milieu' where we are living, here and now, should therefore cause it from the start to appear all of a sudden in a trap, through a short-circuit of the immediate at the heart of the mediation by provoking unexpected access—a haiku,

a metaphor or a beating with a stick; or in that subterfuge of involuntary memory. In the indentation
which is then opened up, a strategy is sketched out
which leads us out of hazard, an ethic becomes possible which dispenses with the codifications of morality. There is no further need to divide the world in
two or to postulate another reality. A veil has suddenly
been slipped off, an illusion caused by a sequence has
burst open, but without for all that revealing something else for us—this immediate is crumbling and
even revealed to be immense or, rather, absolute,
claiming nothing other, simply by the fact that we
have to know how to draw alongside it.

Let us recall the stages of this new knowledge
elevating 'living' into a strategy. Let us begin by
renouncing the *postponement*, so as to make a *moment*
emerge, while allowing it to come (to ripen) from the
moment thanks to the *deferred* (1). Let us choose to
rise up from what is settled to the springing up, or
from the comfortable platitude of the determination
of the *effective* which has left it—let us not allow
living to *coincide* with any inherent property (2). Let
us decide to put an end to the prestige of the End so
as to give a place to the 'between' of the holding-
between[20]—living is fulfilled in this *between* which
allows a grasp, and not by its extremities (3). Let us

think of this 'living' without refraining from the concept, but in the crux of a conceptual contradiction
which diverges it within itself by disclosing and tight-
ening it (4). Finally let us not give in to the illusion
of an initial immediacy, but, similarly, cut loose the
mediation from the immediate, so as not to allow it
to be indefinitely postponed (5). These are so many
conditions of 'awakening', but without conversion,
since the one appears fully through the other and this
internal day is enough to cause the absolute to spring
up under its oblique rays. This runs counter to any
light which comes from an Outside, from above, and
is cast downwards, something which, on the contrary,
flattens and renders it *settled*.

Heraclitus had already named the 'awakenings' as
oi egerthentes, against the 'mass' who did not 'think'
things 'as they encountered them' but shut themselves
in the sequence of their internal film and who while
'present are absent'—not 'awakening' to the here and
now. These people are at once present and absent,
living in a mixture of both one and the other, neither
really present nor confronting absence. Likewise, they
neither know how to take advantage of the absence to
cross over so as to enable presence to emerge, nor how
to cause the full to spring forth from the hollow—
they do not know how to make *evidence* prominent

through *withdrawal*. The 'awakened', on the other hand, are those who deploy contrasts, make divergences work, at the same time as they communicate from within, up to their *foundations of ambiguity*. They, likewise, render the world to its springing up and so enable a 'rising up'. They can equally well be called the *Matinaux* (René Char[21]). In order for 'living' to be strategically precipitated outside of its torpor and deadlock, and from what it then newly allows as crossing, as transposition, the one illuminating itself in the other, a *trans-parency* arises which no longer doubts its appearance and alone can give *access*.

We would then no longer have to dream about 'true life', the beyond, or of dividing life into two. We would equally not be afraid of being passed aside.

NOTES

1 Through the use of the partitive, here, the author wishes to emphasize that this is referring to the essence to the tree or the field, not simply a specific tree or field. [Trans]

2 In French, 'maintenant' means both 'now' and 'maintaining'. [Trans]

3 Pierre Leyris and François Houan translate by poetizing, 'The great Vase is slow to perfect' (2009: 101), as does D. C. Lau. 'The Great Vessel takes long to complete' (see Lao-Tzu 1992: 102).

4 When we think that in 1943 Heidegger undertook to translate the *Laozi* into German with the aid of a Chinese friend, but that he was stopped along the way . . . because it was becoming German.

5 'Hence Christianity marks a *progress* in psychological perspicacity: La Rochefoucauld and Pascal. It has understood *the essential identity of human actions* and their fundamental equivalences' (Nietzsche).

6 Throughout this paragraph, Jullien is playing on the different meanings of *entretien* as 'maintenance' and 'conversation, interview', but also *entre-tien* (between yours) and *entre-tient* (held between). [Trans]

7 Referring to the Enlightenment group around the philosopher Baron d'Holbach (1723–89) which regularly met during the years from 1750 to 1780. [Trans]

8 Marie François Xavier Bichat (1771–1802): a French anatomist and physiologist. [Trans]

9 Here and throughout the next passage, Jullien is playing on the fact that Montaigne's essays are also 'attempts' or 'tries' or even 'tests', all of which meanings are contained by the French word *essai*. [Trans]

10 *Schwärmerei*: 'excessive or unwholesome sentiment'. [Trans]

11 *Biais du gars* refers to the artisanal (rural) knowledge of exactly how to accomplish a task that comes through personal experience alone. [Trans]

12 Antiphon (480–411 BCE): Sophist orator and statesman. [Trans]

13 Pierre Hadot (1922–2010): French philosopher specializing in ancient philosophy who advocated a return to the spiritual exercises of the Greeks, by which the practice of philosophy necessarily involves a transformation of the philosopher. [Trans]

14 René Leriche (1879–1955): a pioneering French surgeon. [Trans]

15 In 1991, James Turrell created an installation in Poitiers, in which, over a period of months, 10,000 visitors, dressed in striped turn-of-the-century bathing suits devised by Turrell, were invited to dive into a swimming pool, pass under a separating wall and discover the changing light of the open sky from within an enclosed space. [Trans]

16 A *kalpa* in Indian philosophy is a period between the creation and recreation of a world, generally reckoned at 336 million years. [Trans]

17 Master Ju Zhi: ninth-century Zen master. An anecdote recounts that when he found a student imitating his way of responding to question, he immediately pulled out a knife and cut the student's finger off. [Trans]

18 Linji Yixuan (died 866 CE): founder of a school of Chan Buddhism that became one of the bases of Zen. His teaching involved the use of sometimes violent methods intended to provoke enlightenment. [Trans]

19 The reference is to Proust. [Trans]

20 See also Chapter 3. [Trans]

21 René Char (1907–88): French surrealist poet. one of whose collections is entitled *Les matinaux* ('the morning times' or 'morning ones'), translated into English by Michael Worton as *The Dawn Breakers* (Newcastle upon Tyne: Bloodaxe, 1993). [Trans]

BIBLIOGRAPHY

[Since Jullien's work is so much concerned with translation (or mis-translation) and as often the French translation differs markedly from the available English, we have preferred (especially in relation to classical Greek, Roman and Chinese texts) to translate from the French. The English translations we have used for comparison are nevertheless given below.— Trans]

ARISTOTLE. 1984. *Metaphysics* in the *Complete Works of Aristotle*, VOL. 2 (Jonathan Barnes ed. and trans.). Princeton, NJ: Princeton University Press.

———. 2011. *Nicomachean Ethics* (Robert C. Bartlett and Susan D. Collins trans). Chicago: University of Chicago Press.

AUGUSTINE. 1960. *The Confessions* of *Saint Augustine* (John K. Ryan trans.). New York: Doubleday.

———. 1993. *Tractates on the Gospel of John* (John W. Rettig trans.). Washington, DC: Catholic University of America Press.

BASHŌ MATSUO. 1983. *Le haïkaï selon Bashō: traité de poétique, propos recueillis par ses disciples* (including 'Les Notes de Kyorai', 'Kyorai shô', de Kyorai Mukai, 'Les Trois livres', 'Sanzôshi', de Tohô Hattori et des extraits du 'Sarumino') (René Sieffert ed. and trans.). Paris: Presses orientaliste de France.

BERGSON, Henri. 1984. *La Pensée et le mouvant* in *Œuvres*. Paris: Presses Universitaires de France.

CANGUILHEM, Georges. 1991. *The Normal and the Pathological* (Carolyn R. Fawcett trans.). New York: Zone Books.

———. 2006. 'Aspects du vitalisme' in *La Connaissance et la vie*. Paris: Vrin.

DERRIDA, Jacques. 1981. *Dissemination* (Barbara Johnson trans.). Chicago: University of Chicago Press.

DESCARTES, René. 1970. *Philosophical Letters* (Anthony Kenny ed. and trans.). Oxford: Clarendon Press.

———. 1989. *The Passions of the Soul* (Stephen Voss trans.). Indiana: Hackett.

DIXSAUT, Monique (ed.). 1999. *Le Fêlure du plaisir: études sur le 'Philèbe' de Platon*. Paris: Vrin.

FREUD, Sigmund. 1961. *Civilisation and Its Discontents* (James Strachey trans.). New York: W. W. Norton.

GREGORY OF NYSSA. 1978. *The Life of Moses* (Abraham J. Malherbe and Everett Ferguson trans). Mahwah, NJ: Paulist Press.

GUO QINGFAN (ed.). 1983. *Xiaozheng Zhuangzi*. Taipei: Shijie shuju.

HARL, Marguerite. 1993. *Le déchiffrement du sens; études sur l'herméneutique chrétienne d'Origène à Grégoire de Nysse*. Paris: Institut d'études augustiniennes.

HEGEL, Georg Wilhelm Friedrich. 1977. *Phenomenology of Spirit* (A.V. Miller trans.). Oxford: Clarendon Press.

HEIDEGGER, Martin. 1939. *Vom Wesen und Begriff der* physis. *Aristoteles, Physik B, 1*. Frankfurt am Main: Vittorio Klostermann.

———. 1957a. 'Die Sichentziehen ist die Weise, wie Sein west, d.h. als An-wesen sich zuschickt' in *Der Satz vom Grund*. Neske: Pfullingen.

———. 1957b. *Identität und Differenz*. Stuttgart: Klett-Cotta.

———. 1965. *Vom Wesen des Grundes*. Frankfurt am Main: Vittorio Klostermann.

———. 1976. 'Das Ende der Philosophie und die Aufgabe des Denkens' in *Zur. Sache des Denkens*. Tübingen: Max Niemeyer.

———. 1998. *Was ist Metaphysik?* Frankfurt am Main: Vittorio Klostermann.

HERACLITUS OF EPHESUS. 2003. *Fragments* (Brooks Haxton trans.). New York: Penguin Books.

HORACE. 2001. *The Epistles* (David Ferry trans.). New York: Farrar, Straus and Giroux.

HUSSERL, Edmund. 1964. *Phenomenology of Internal Time Consciousness* (James S. Churchill and Calvin O. Schrag trans). Bloomington: Indiana University Press.

———. 1977. *Cartesian Meditations: An Introduction to Phenomenology* (Dorion Cairns trans.). Dordrecht and Boston: Kluwer Academic Publishers.

———. 1991. *On the Phenomenology of the Consciousness of Internal Time (1893–1917)* (John Barnett Brough trans.). Dordrecht and Boston: Kluwer Academic Publishers.

HYPPOLITE, Jean. 1974. *Genesis and Structure of Hegel's 'Phenomenology of Spirit'* (Samuel Cherniak and John Heckman trans). Evanston, IL: Northwestern University Press.

JACOBI, Friedrich Heinrich. 2000. *David Hume et la croyance* (Louis Guillermit trans.). Paris: Vrin.

JULLIEN, François. 2001. *Du 'temps', éléments d'une philosophie du vivre.* Paris: Grasset.

———. 2006. *Si parler va sans dire. Du logos et autres resources.* Paris: Édition du Seuil.

KANT, Immanuel. 1978. *The Critique of Judgement* (James Creed Meredith trans.). Oxford: Clarendon Press.

LAO-TZEU. 2009. *La Voie et sa vertu* (Pierre Leyris & François Houang trans). Paris: Édition du Seuil.

LAO-TZU. 1992. *Te-Tao Ching: A New Translation Based on the Recently Discovered Ma-wang-tui Texts* (Robert G. Henricks trans.). New York: Ballantine Books.

LUCRETIUS. 2007. *The Nature of Things* (Alicia Stallings trans.). Harmondsworth: Penguin Books.

MALLARMÉ, Stéphane. 1994. *Collected Poems: A Bilingual Edition* (Henry Weinfield trans.). Berkeley: University of California Press.

MARCUS AURELIUS. 1990a. *The Meditations of Marcus Aurelius* (A. S. L. Farquharson trans.). New York: Oxford University Press.

———. 1990b. *A Selection from the Letters of Marcus and Fronto* (R. B. Rutherford trans.). New York: Oxford University Press.

MENCIUS. 1963. *Mencius: A New Translation Arranged and Annotated for the General Reader by W. A. C. H. Dobson.* London: Oxford University Press.

MERLEAU-PONTY, Maurice. 1968. *The Visible and the Invisible, Fllowed by Working Notes* (Alphonso Lingis trans.). Evanston, IL: Northwestern University Press.

MONTAIGNE, Michel de. 1987. *The Essays* (M. A. Screech trans.). Harmondsworth: Penguin Books.

NIETZSCHE, Friedrich. 1961. *Thus Spoke Zarathustra* (R. J. Hollingdale trans.). Harmondsworth: Penguin Books.

————. 1968a. *Beyond Good and Evil: Prelude to a Philosophy of the Future* (Walter Kaufmann trans.) in *The Basic Writings of Nietzsche*. New York: The New Library.

————. 1968b. *The Will to Power* (Walter Kaufmann and R. J. Hollingdale trans). New York: Vintage Books.

————. 1974. *The Gay Science: With a Prelude in Rhymes and an Appendix of Songs* (Walter Kaufmann trans.). New York: Vintage Books.

PARMENIDES OF ELEA. 1984. *Fragments: A Text and Translation with an Introduction by David Gallop*. Toronto: University of Toronto Press.

PASCAL, Blaise. 1966. *Pensées* (A. J. Krailsheimer trans.). Harmondsworth: Penguin Books.

PLATO. 1931. *Philebus* in *The Dialogues of Plato, Volume 4* (Benjamin Jowett trans.). London: Oxford University Press. Available at: http://oll.libertyfund.org/titles/768 (last accessed on 2 October 2015).

————. 1961a. *Theaetetus* (F. M. Crawford trans.) in *The Collected Dialogues of Plato* (Edith Hamilton and Huntington Cairns eds, Lane Cooper trans.). Princeton, NJ: Princeton University Press.

————. 1961b. *Phaedo* (Hugh Tredernich trans.) in *The Collected Dialogues of Plato*. Princeton, NJ: Princeton University Press.

——. 1961c. *Phaedrus* (R. Hackforth trans.) in *The Collected Dialogues of Plato*. Princeton, NJ: Princeton University Press.

——. 1961d. *The Sophist* (F. M. Crawford trans.) in *The Collected Dialogues of Plato*. Princeton, NJ: Princeton University Press.

——. 1961e. *The Republic* (Paul Shorey trans.) in *The Collected Dialogues of Plato*. Princeton, NJ: Princeton University Press.

——. 2009. *Gorgias* (Robin Waterfield trans.). New York: Oxford University Press.

PROUST, Marcel. 1992a. *In Search of Lost Time, Volume 1: Swann's Way* (C. K. Scott-Moncrieff trans. and D. J. Enright rev.). London: Chatto and Windus.

——. 1992b. *In Search of Lost Time, Volume 7: Time Regained* (Andreas Mayor trans. and D. J. Enright rev.). London: Chatto and Windus.

ROUSSEAU, Jean-Jacques. 2008. *Confessions* (Patrick Coleman ed. and Angela Scholar trans.). New York: Oxford University Press.

——. 2011. *Reveries of the Solitary Walker* (Russell Goulbourne trans.). New York: Oxford University Press.

WANG WEI. n.d. 'Lin hu tung' in *Wang Youcheng Ji janzhu*. Zhong hua shuju.

ACKNOWLEDGEMENTS

The translators would like to thank Robin Weichart,
Liliana Albertazzi and François Jullien for all their
help in determining the correct and/or most appropriate
English terms for some of the more difficult expressions
contained in the text.